P9-CCW-754

Lord, blow . . . I join thousands in praying that at this very moment, which Satan means for hindering the mission of the King to the nations, God will turn it all for strategic advance. May God use this book to enable thousands to see that God is on the move in our generation. And may the Lord madden the evil one by turning his tactical ripples against the kingdom into a tidal wave of Great Commission completion.

John Piper, founder, desiringGod.org,
author of *Desiring God* and *Don't Waste Your Life*

In *What Are You Going to Do with Your Life?*, Pastor J. D. reminds us that there is nothing more vital or fulfilling than pursuing the purpose and plan Jesus has for each one of us. God has invited us to be his co-laborers in this world in a myriad of different ways. There is no one-size-fits-all approach to disciple making, but there is one call for all disciples of Jesus. We have the opportunity to live out an adventure that will make our lives count for eternity, to settle for anything less would be tragic. If you really want to change the world, this book is for you.

Christine Caine, founder A21 and Propel Women

Inspirational. The day Dr. John Piper gave his talk at Passion OneDay 2000 was a transformational moment like few others I have experienced. Since that day, many have been challenged and convinced to live their lives for what matters most. My friend, Pastor J. D. Greear, has expounded upon that idea and is calling today's generation to leverage their lives for the glory, the fame, and the renown of our God. I am confident that *What Are You*

Going to Do with Your Life? will be a book many of us will never forget.

> **Louie Giglio**, pastor of Passion City Church, founder of Passion Conferences, and author of *Not Forsaken*

What are you going to do with your life?

What are you going to do with your life?

J.D.
Greear

B&H
PUBLISHING
NASHVILLE, TENNESSEE

Copyright © 2020 by J. D. Greear
All rights reserved.
Printed in the United States of America

978-1-0877-0929-1

Published by B&H Publishing Group
Nashville, Tennessee

Dewey Decimal Classification: 248.84
Subject Heading: CHRISTIAN LIFE /
DISCIPLESHIP / SELF-PERCEPTION

Unless otherwise noted, all Scripture quotations are taken from
the Christian Standard Bible®, Copyright © 2017 by Holman Bible
Publishers. Used by permission. Christian Standard Bible® and CSB®
are federally registered trademarks of Holman Bible Publishers.

Also used: English Standard Version (ESV), ESV® Text
Edition: 2016. Copyright © 2001 by Crossway Bibles,
a publishing ministry of Good News Publishers.

Also used: New King James Version (NKJV), copyright
© 1982 by Thomas Nelson. Used by permission.

Cover Design by Christi Kearney.

It is the Publisher's goal to minimize disruption caused by
technical errors or invalid websites. While all links are active at
the time of publication, because of the dynamic nature of the
internet, some web addresses or links contained in this book
may have changed and may no longer be valid. B&H Publishing
Group bears no responsibility for the continuity or content of
the external site, nor for that of subsequent links. Contact the
external site for answers to questions regarding its content.

2 3 4 5 6 7 8 • 25 24 23 22 21

To Dave Turner and Wes Smith, who not only champion this message but have trained hundreds of others to live it out. It seems like everywhere in the world I go, I meet someone who is there because of your influence.

Contents

Foreword

Correctly answering the question on the cover of this book is critical to whether or not your life is going to count in this world. I make this statement without hesitation or reservation, and every word in this statement matters.

By "whether or not your life is going to count in this world," I mean to say that your life may not count in this world. At least not for what matters. In my Bible reading just a few days ago, I read the story of the rich man who asked Jesus what he must do to inherit eternal life. Jesus, "looking at him, loved him and said to him, 'You lack one thing: go, sell all that you have and give to the poor, and you will have treasure in heaven; and come, follow me.'" In that moment, this man had a choice. Was his life going to count for what matters: care for the poor, treasure in heaven, and a life of following Jesus? Or was his life going to count for what doesn't matter: riches for himself, treasures on earth, and a life of forsaking Jesus? He chose the latter, and he squandered his life.

It's possible for you or I to squander our lives in the same way, for we have the same choice. We can love those in need or ignore those in need. We can live for treasures on earth or treasures in heaven. We can forsake or follow Jesus.

That last phrase—"to forsake or follow Jesus"—is the crux of the choice we have, and it's why I say "correctly answering the question on the cover of this book is critical." Many people, when they read the question, "What are you going to do with your life?" think, *There's no correct answer to that question. The course of my life is specific to me and up to me to determine.*

But that's not true if you're a follower of Jesus. To be a Christian means that you have surrendered the right to determine the course of your life. Now to be clear, that's not the common picture of Christianity, at least not in America. To be a Christian in America means you go through certain religious rituals and call yourself a Christian, all while living however you want to live.

But that's not a Christian according to Christ. Based upon his Word, to be a Christian means you have died to yourself, your ideas, and your dreams for your life. To be a Christian according to Christ means that you have lost your life as you knew it, and you have found new life in him, which means you now live with his ideas and his dreams for your life.

Moreover, Jesus has made those ideas and dreams clearly known for your life, and they are not specific to you. Love God with all your heart, soul, mind, and strength. Love your neighbor as yourself. Make disciples of all the nations. Spend your life spreading the gospel of God for the glory of God. For the follower of Jesus, these plans are unequivocally and unquestionably what Jesus has designed for your life.

Now obviously Jesus' plans for all of us will play out differently in each of our lives. We are all called and gifted differently, and that's not accidental. However, the trajectory of our lives is fundamentally the same, whether we are gifted as entrepreneurs, painters, or pastors. For every follower of Jesus, his commandments, commission, and cause will (and must) dictate every decision we make in life, from who we marry to where we go to school to what career path we take to where we live to how we retire (or not).

That's what this book is about. It's about asking the question on the cover of this book and answering that question not according to our ways in this world, but according to God's truth in his Word. It's about helping every follower of Jesus, from the student to the senior adult and everyone in between, realize that our lives are a mist, and we all only have a little bit of time left. In light of this reality, this book is about helping you and me make the mist we have on this earth count for what matters most in eternity.

David Platt

"What we do in life echoes in eternity."
—Maximus Decimus Meridius, *GLADIATOR*

Chapter 1

Don't Waste Your Life

Early in the afternoon on May 20, 2000, in a large field on a farm outside Memphis, Tennessee, a preacher in his mid-fifties, dressed in his signature herringbone sport coat and black tie, took his place behind a lectern to address a crowd of more than 40,000 college students.

The air was chilly, the wind brisk, and a light rain had begun to fall. The crowd of students was restless. They had already sat through a packed slate of morning sessions. To escape the damp, students held their rain jackets over their heads. Several used the moment to get up and go for a walk or go back to their tents.

Not an auspicious beginning for a generation-defining moment.

The speaker, understandably, looked a little flustered. He was trying to shield the temperamental mic from the whipping wind with one hand and hold down his notes with the other. And just a few minutes into his sermon, a gust of wind blew half of his notes off of the lectern and into the crowd.

The message was not going well. The man quietly prayed: *"Father in heaven, you know how inadequate I feel at this moment. And so I ask for a very special anointing and help from you."*

He took a deep breath, and then, leaning down on the lectern, pinning his remaining notes down with his arm, said:

> "Three weeks ago we got word at our church that Ruby Eliason and Laura Edwards had both been killed in Cameroon," he began. "Ruby was over eighty. Single all her life, she poured it out for one great thing: to make Jesus Christ known among the unreached, the poor, and the sick. Laura was a widow, a medical doctor, pushing eighty years old, and serving at Ruby's side in Cameroon. The brakes failed, the car went over the cliff, and they were both killed instantly. And I asked my people: Was that a tragedy?"

Students responded, "No!"

"No," the preacher echoed. "That is a glory. I'll tell you what a tragedy is."

He then pulled out a page from *Reader's Digest* and read,

> "Bob and Penny took . . . early retirement from their jobs in the Northeast five years ago when he was 59 and she was 51. Now they live in Punta Gorda, Florida, where they cruise on their 30-foot trawler, play softball, and collect shells."

He continued:

> "The American Dream: come to the end of your
> life—*your one and only life*—and let the last
> great work before you give an account to your
> Creator be, 'I collected shells. See my shells.'
> *That* is a tragedy. People today are spending bil-
> lions of dollars to persuade you to embrace that
> tragic dream. And I get forty minutes to plead
> with you: don't buy it. *Don't waste your life.*"[1]

Don't waste your life.

John Piper was the preacher, and this sermon became known as his "seashell sermon." Students began passing it on to others. Eventually, it seemed, my whole generation of Christian students had heard it.

Sarah Zylstra, writing for The Gospel Coalition, notes that a staggering amount of today's leaders point back to that message as a pivotal moment in their lives. David Platt said the message fundamentally redefined how he looked at life. Matt Carter, lead pastor of Sagemont Church, Houston, Texas, said: "I was in the crowd. That sermon ended all my dreams of retirement."[2] Trevin Wax, senior vice president of Theology and Communications at LifeWay Christian Resources, talks about being wrecked by Piper's powerful illustration of a "wasted" life in retirement.[3] Marian Jordan Ellis, now a popular Bible teacher and author, was then a brand-new Christian. She said, "[Piper's poem] literally rang in my ears for 15 years."[4]

As for me, I had just returned from serving for two years as a missionary in Southeast Asia. I was trying to figure out what God wanted with the rest of my life. I could feel the allures of comfort, stability, and the American Dream calling my name. Piper's message hit my heart like a lightning bolt.

Don't waste your life.

The phrase still haunts me.

The idea is simple: Eternity is real. The gospel is true. People's souls matter. Your life counts. Don't waste it.

In 2003, the message made it to print with the book *Don't Waste Your Life*. To date, that book has sold more than 600,000 copies.[5]

Asking the Wrong Question?

I was a junior in college when I realized that, though I had been a Christian for several years, I'd never asked God the one question he wanted me to ask about my life. I'd been asking him *if* he wanted to use me to make an impact for his kingdom. The question should not have been *if*, only where and how.

My pastor had challenged me to read through the book of Romans seven times that year. I was on my last time through when Romans 2:12 seemed to lift off the page:

> For all who have sinned without the law will also
> perish without the law, and all who have sinned
> under the law will be judged by the law. (ESV)

That verse means that even those who haven't heard the gospel are still under God's judgment because each of us has a "law" written on our hearts, a law that we all, without exception, have disobeyed. Our only hope for salvation is a special act of grace, which God gives through the message about Christ.

It's not that I hadn't understood that before, but that morning its meaning poured over my heart like a flood. The lostness of the world pressed in on my heart with an intensity I thought might crush me. I sat in silence for several moments. Tears came. I felt like I couldn't speak. Finally, I whispered, "Lord, if you will let me go and tell them, I'll go. Will you let me go?"

In that moment, it seemed like the Spirit of God whispered to me, "Now, at last, you're asking the *right* question."

You see, up until that moment my attitude had been, "If God wants something from me in his kingdom, he'll let me know." And barring some special instruction, I assumed his expectation of me was to find some career that suited me, do it well, go to church, tithe, and stay out of trouble.

That morning I realized that the lostness of the world and urgency of the gospel demand a different response. A vision came into my mind. I was walking alongside a set of railroad tracks when I noticed a small child stranded on them. In the distance, I could hear a freight train headed right toward him. I knew that in such a moment, I wouldn't calmly get down on my knees and say, "Oh God, if you want me to do something, just let me know," and then wait for some special instruction from heaven. I would know God's will in that moment without even asking: *save the child*.

Here's the reality: people in the world without Jesus are headed toward a tragedy every bit as real and ten billion times more devastating than a child stranded on railroad tracks. God has told us it is his will that none of them should perish, and in order for that to happen, they *must* hear the gospel. "The Lord is . . . not willing," Peter said, "that any should perish but all [would] come to repentance" (2 Pet. 3:9 NKJV).

We talk about "finding the will of God." In reality, it's never been lost! It's spelled out right there in that verse. God wants every person alive to hear the gospel, and he uses his church to make that happen.

That morning I got a glimpse of the lostness of the world and could only cry out, like the prophet Isaiah had so many years before me, "Here I am. Send me" (Isa. 6:8). *Every* Christian who catches a glimpse of the lostness of the world and the greatness of God's offer of salvation should respond that way.

The right question, you see, is not *if* God has called you to his mission, only *where.*

As we'll discuss later in this book, calling is not a sacred privilege reserved for a select few, conveyed through some mystical manifestation. The call to leverage your life for the Great Commission was *included* in the call to follow Jesus: "Follow me," he told them, "and I will make you fish for people" (Matt. 4:19).

So you can stop waiting on a mystical moment, a wet fleece, or a quiver in your liver. You're called.

You don't need to wait on a voice. He's given you a verse.

A Restless Generation

It has been two decades since Piper issued that fateful challenge. I write this book because it's time for a new generation of

Christians to hear it—and to say to God, "Here I am, send me." To consider what Jesus' promises about the gospel and his warnings about eternity mean for how we order our lives.

This generation is a restless one. You have been the beneficiaries of greater technological advance and wealth acquisition than any generation in history, but still you know something's not right.

Quarterback Tom Brady may have summed it up best. After winning his third Super Bowl, he was asked by Steve Kroft in an interview on *60 Minutes*: "[This] whole upward trajectory—what have you learned about yourself? . . ."

Brady answered,

> ". . . Why do I have three Super Bowl rings, and still think there's something greater out there for me? I mean maybe a lot of people would say, 'Hey man, this is what it is.' I reached my goal, my dream, my life. Me, I think: God, it's gotta be more than this. . . . And what else is there for me?"
>
> Kroft asked, "What's the answer?"
>
> Brady smiled for a moment, then the smile faded. "I wish I knew," he said. "I wish I knew."[6]

Another of our generation's greatest philosophical minds, comedian Jim Carrey, said the same: "I think everybody should get rich and famous and do everything they ever dreamed of so they can see that it's not the answer."[7]

Many look for a global cause to give their lives to, thinking the fulfilled life is one that empowers the poor or saves the planet. Phrases like "social consciousness" and "tolerance" now describe a well-lived life or well-managed corporation. We want to eradicate poverty. Extend human rights. End global warming. Save the planet from plastic straws.

I read recently that college graduates rate helping others and providing aid to those in need among their top post-college aspirations. One study found "living with purpose" to be the number one thing high school students want out of life—above money, fame, and even a happy marriage. Another survey asked twentysomethings, "What would make for a dream job?" I expected the top answer to be about money, or maybe influence and fame. And yes, money was on there—but it only came in at 24 percent. The top answer (nearly double that of money) was, "Feeling passionate about my work."[8]

Translation: "I want to live for something that matters."

We want our lives to *count*. If we are asked, "What are you going to do with your life?" we want to be able to answer in a way that shows our life has some significance.

That is a yearning put into us by God. And many of those causes are good and worthy ones.

But for the Christian, there is one cause that should outweigh them all.

If what Jesus said was true, what determines a person's eternal future is whether or not they know him.

"I am the way, the truth, and the life. No
one comes to the Father except through me."
(John 14:6)

The gospel declares that Jesus died so that people from every
nation, every culture, and every language on earth could know
his salvation and find in him the joy of living. He has offered his
salvation to all who will receive it in him. The apostle John says:

But as many as received Him, to them He gave
the right to become children of God, to those
who believe in His name. (John 1:12 NKJV)

But in order to receive him, they have to hear about him.
Paul explains:

How, then, can they call on him they have not
believed in? And how can they believe without
hearing about him? And how can they hear
without a preacher? And how can they preach
unless they are sent? (Rom. 10:14–15)

I know for many of us this raises a lot of questions—questions that we'll get to later in this book. But for now, just know
that for someone who takes the Bible seriously, the gospel is the
most important cause of all.

As John Piper says, relieving any type of suffering is a good
and worthy goal. But the worst kind of suffering—the kind that
deserves our most earnest attention—is *eternal* suffering.

> Suffering in this world is terrible and limited,
> but suffering in the next world is terrible and
> eternal. And love sees it that way. Love does not
> shut its eyes to this world or that world. Love
> reckons with the reality of suffering here, and
> the worse reality of suffering there.[9]

If the Bible is true, then a life that matters must take the realities of eternal suffering into account.

"All This I've Done for You. What Have You Done for Me?"

I am guessing that you've never heard of Nicolaus Ludwig von Zinzendorf. And I'm guessing that if you have, you probably won't name any of your kids after him. If you already did, put down this book right now and go apologize to them.

But, if you live in the Western world, he's a more important part of your Christian heritage than you may realize. Born into a noble family in Dresden, Germany, in 1700, "Count" Zinzendorf grew up with the expectation that he would take over his family's wealthy estate. Being a "count" in those days meant that you basically did very little and got lots of money for it. His life was destined to be one of leisure, pleasure, and prestige. A life of seashells.

In 1720, as the young count toured an art museum in Dusseldorf, he was gripped by Domenico Feti's painting, *Ecce Homo* ("Behold the man!"), which depicts Jesus just moments before the crucifixion. Beaten, bloodied, wearing a crown of thorns. Inscribed below Jesus are the words: *"All this I have done for you. What have you done for me?"*[10]

In a moment similar to what I experienced reading Romans 2, God gripped Count Zinzendorf's heart with the brevity of life, the reality of lostness, and the urgency of the gospel. In that moment, Count Z knew that he could no longer pursue a life of leisure.

He began leveraging his estate as a staging ground for God's mission, donating his resources to sponsor mission ventures all over the globe. Hundreds of young twentysomethings came from around Germany to be trained in the gospel and sent out on mission. They called themselves "Moravians," named for the place from which many of them originated.

One night in 1727 Zinzendorf's small gospel community prayed through the night, asking God to use their movement to reshape the world with the gospel. They literally never stopped. And I mean that. Morning came, and they began to pray in shifts, around the clock. That night birthed what has been called the "hundred-year prayer meeting," a round-the-clock prayer chain that continued for more than a century.

From that prayer movement God raised up a generation to plant churches and establish gospel communities from Greenland to Guyana, from Jamaica to Cape Town, and from New York to North Carolina.

This movement did not consist of only vocational pastors, either. So-called "ordinary" believers caught the vision. Moravians formed for-profit trading companies that enabled them to carry the gospel into difficult places. As we'll see later in this book, business can take the gospel to places that "mission trips" can never get to. In fact, historians say the most successful and enduring of the Moravian mission works were those established by the trading companies, not the mission boards.[11]

A few Moravians even moved to the place where I would one day grow up—Winston-Salem, North Carolina—to establish a gospel community there. Their gospel impact would shape the community I grew up in. My home church was located less than a mile from the Moravian gospel outpost they established in 1753.

Zinzendorf penned words that defined the movement:

> I have but one passion—it is He, it is He alone.
> The world is the field and the field is the world;
> and henceforth that country shall be my home
> where I can be most used in winning souls for
> Christ. . . *I desire only to preach the gospel, die,
> and be forgotten.*[12]

Forgotten in time, maybe. But with lives still echoing in eternity.

Only One Life to Live, 'Twill Soon Be Past

Years later, another unlikely man would be gripped by the same vision that captivated Zinzendorf. His name was C. T. Studd, and he was England's most famous cricketer. (For Americans, we may not think of "cricket champ" as a terribly impressive achievement. But in the nineteenth century, cricket was the world's most popular sport, and Studd was its Lebron

James. And for the record, if you are going to be a professional athlete, you can't get much better of a name than "Studd.")

At the height of his career, when he was the star of England's national team, Studd couldn't shake the thought that his life was yielding little eternal value. So he did the unthinkable: he resigned the team and left to spread the gospel in China, India, and eventually the Belgian Congo, where he died. Imagine Lebron James holding a press conference this afternoon and announcing that he was "taking his talents to Siberia" because people there need to hear about Jesus.

Naturally, people all over the world asked Studd why he would do such a thing. His response:

> If Jesus Christ be God and died for me, then
> no sacrifice can be too great for me to make for
> Him.[13]

Can't you hear in that the echo of Zinzendorf's words? Studd later wrote a poem that encapsulated his new outlook on life, a poem that John Piper would reference on that chilly May afternoon in Memphis before 40,000 American college students:

> I grew up in a home where my father spent
> himself as an evangelist to bring the gospel of
> Jesus Christ to the lost. He had one consuming
> vision: preach the gospel. There was a plaque in
> our kitchen for all my growing up years. Now
> it hangs in our living room. I have looked at it
> almost daily for about forty-eight years.[14]

The line from Studd's poem?

> *"Only one life, 'twill soon be past; only what's done*
> *for Christ will last."*[15]

Alas, I'm not a college student anymore. Life has moved fast. Sometimes I can't fathom where the time went, how quickly life has gone by. Like a roll of toilet paper, every revolution seems to go faster. Not the most elegant example, I know. But I feel like just yesterday I was enrolling myself as a student in college. Today, I have a daughter preparing to do so. Soon enough, her daughter will be. And then it will all be over.

This life will soon be past. What have I done for Christ that will last?

Will I look back with regret at how I used my life? Will I feel like I wasted it?

One day your life will draw to a close, too. It's a morbid thought, I know, but you really need to think about it. Because that day may be today, or it may come ten, fifty, or even eighty years from now. But it's coming. (Last time I checked, the death rate in America is holding steady at 100 percent.)

When that day comes, will you regret what you did with your life?

What will you take with you into eternity? A nice house? A solid investment portfolio? A few worthless Super Bowl rings?

Seashells?

How many of those things that occupy so much of your energy, time, and focus will you actually keep forever?

One hundred years from now, how will you wish you had used your life? How about 10,000 years from now? Wisdom begins by viewing your life from the end and acting in a way *now* that you know *then* you'll be glad you did.

Only one life, 'twill soon be past; only what's done for Christ will last.

Jim Elliot, missionary to Ecuador, who would be martyred there only three years after he arrived, said it best: "He is no fool who gives what he cannot keep to gain that which he cannot lose."[16]

In this book, I want to convince you to give up those things you cannot keep in order to gain those things you cannot lose, too.

I want to encourage you to reckon with what you really believe about Jesus, his promises, and eternity. I want to challenge you to re-examine your life in light of them. And I want to plead with you to not waste your life.

If you are a college student, I want to challenge you to make decisions about where you are going and what you plan to do with eternity in view.

If you are nearing retirement, I want to encourage you to make this next chapter of your life count—to not waste it picking up seashells or touring golf resorts. Do you really want to spend the last fifteen years of your life before you meet Jesus *on vacation*? How will you explain to him that you used the most unencumbered chapter of your life in leisure, living for yourself?

And if you are somewhere in between, I want to challenge you to consider how you might leverage your career and your resources for the gospel now, and to make plans for how you can do so in even greater ways in the future.

I am writing this book because we need another generation who desires only to preach the gospel, die, and be forgotten. To consider the question that so haunted Zinzendorf: *"All this I have done for you. What have you done for me?"*

Ask yourself: *Where would I be had Jesus not come for me? Had he chosen to stay in heaven and enjoy the privileges of the throne?* The sobering answer: *exactly the same place people all over the world are without you.* The gospel has to be heard to be believed. As Martin Luther said, it wouldn't matter if Jesus died one thousand times if nobody ever heard about it.

Life is too short, eternity is too long, and the stakes too high to waste your years.

> *Only one life, yes only one,*
> *Now let me say, "Thy will be done";*
>
> *And when at last I'll hear the call,*
> *I know I'll say "'twas worth it all";*
>
> *Only one life, 'twill soon be past,*
> *Only what's done for Christ will last.*[17]

One thing I am sure of: If you are reading this book, God has a role for you in his kingdom.

Life is short. Eternity is forever. We only get a brief moment in time to use the former to transform the latter.

Don't waste it.

Chapter 2

Kick Your Bucket List

"The wisest moments in life are the ones you
live with the final moment in mind."
—Dave Turner, College and Discipleship Pastor,
The Summit Church

Only four experiences in my life have fully lived up to my expectations. That's probably because I tend to overhype things. ("Easily excitable" is what I think the doctor wrote on the Ritalin prescription.)

Nonetheless, many of the things I anticipated most left me with the feeling that they could have been better.

The handful that lived up to expectations?

1. Becoming a Christian
2. Marrying Veronica and having children

(These were both more enjoyable *and* more challenging than I ever imagined.)

Beyond that, the list is pretty short:

3. Visiting Kauai, Hawaii
4. Skydiving

And . . . well, that's it.

I'll bet that a few more experiences would make the list if I ever get a chance to do them. Hiking the Inca trail. Climbing Mt. Everest. Hang-gliding. Flying to the moon.

Experiences like these often get put on a "bucket list." The term "bucket list" became public parlance in 2007 because of a movie by the same name. Morgan Freeman and Jack Nicholson play two unlikely and hilarious friends bonding over their terminal diagnoses, and they make a list of all sorts of crazy adventures they want to go on before they "kick the bucket." They call it their "bucket list."

More recently, the bucket list has been supplanted by YOLO, a four-letter acronym you use to justify some rash and crazy decision. *You Only Live Once,* so live every moment to the fullest! Take advantage of every opportunity. You'll never get a chance to experience this life again, so make sure you get everything out of it that you can.

I will admit, saying YOLO to myself when considering whether to go skydiving felt motivating, and making a bucket list of things I'd like to get to before I die was a fun exercise. But does a bucket list even make sense for a Christian?

How could it?

YOLO is not true.

YALF is. (You actually live forever.)

Bucket lists are inappropriate for Christians not because good Christians stay at home, and settle for a safe, boring life. It's just that we know that life on earth is not our only chance (or even our best chance) to experience what the world has to offer.

Scripture gives every indication that the "new heavens and new earth" (Rev. 21:1, 4) will contain better versions of anything in God's good creation that we enjoyed down here.

Many people wrongly think of heaven as some ethereal life of leisure where saints sit around in diapers on colorless clouds with Nerf bows and arrows, strumming their harps and sipping non-alcoholic piña coladas. We gather at least twice daily for choir practice, but that's our only real activity.

The Bible describes heaven much differently. Though it leaves a lot unsaid, what it does say indicates that heaven is a reality that is *more than,* not less than, anything we experience on earth.

Scholars say "new heaven and new earth" is better read *"renewed heaven and earth."* In other words, the new earth is not a *replacement* of the old, but a renewed and restored version of it, freed from the curse of sin, supercharged with the glory of God. As New Testament scholar N. T. Wright puts it, "God's plan is not to abandon this world, the world which he said was 'very good.' Rather, he intends to remake it. And when he does he will raise all his people to new bodily life to live in it. That is the promise of the Christian gospel."[1]

That all the mountains, rivers, oceans, animals, culture, arts, music, architecture, solar systems, and even extreme sports that I never got to experience here are waiting for me there, in glorified form.

Furthermore, the apostle John goes on to say that God "will bring the glory and honor of the nations into [heaven]" (Rev. 21:26). That means the best of culture—the best of Italian food, the best of Arabian and Colonial architecture, the best art, Mardi Gras (without the debauchery), Walt Disney World (without the lines), the Jersey Shore (without, you know, the Jersey).

(By the way—I can't prove this, but I'm pretty sure that in heaven all the foods that are bad for you here are good for you there, and vice versa. There, ice cream and chocolate are good for the waistline, while cauliflower makes you gain weight. Like I said, I can't prove that, but these things are spiritually discerned. Let the wise reader understand.)

We don't know all that we'll be capable of physically in the resurrection, but Jesus' resurrection is supposed to give us some hints. And, in his resurrected body, Jesus could apparently fly and walk through walls.

I've always wanted to climb Mt. Everest. My wife tells me it's off the table until my kids at least graduate college. And by that time, I may not be physically able, and so I may never get the chance. But that's okay, because in heaven, I'm confident I'll get to climb the renewed one, which will be a lot better anyway. And when I get to the top, I'll fly over to the heavenly Tuscany for dinner.

In cryptic-yet-enticing terms, Paul tells us,

What no eye has seen, no ear has heard, and
no human heart has conceived—God has
prepared these things for those who love him.
(1 Cor. 2:9)

In plain speak, that means that if you can think it, it's not awesome enough. That's pretty fantastic because I can think of some pretty cool things. Heaven likely will have all of them, plus a bunch of other stuff I can't even conceive of yet.

And, of course, this is not even to mention the joy of doing all these things under the watchful and approving eye of an eternally good heavenly Father.

C. S. Lewis depicts that breathtaking moment when believers are translated from this corrupted world to the renewed and restored one with Aslan saying to his children, "Further up and further in!"[2]

And they respond:

I have come home at last! This is my real country! I belong here. This is the land I have been looking for all my life, though I never knew it till now. The reason why we loved the old Narnia is that it sometimes looked a little like this.

Lewis concludes:

All their life in this world and all their adventures had only been the cover and the title page: now at last they were beginning Chapter One

of the Great Story which no one on earth has
read: which goes on forever: in which every
chapter is better than the one before.[3]

So remind me—*why do I need a bucket list*?

There's not anything I'll miss out on down here that I won't
be able to make up in spades up there.

Except.

There is one thing we can't do there that we can do here.

Tell people about Jesus.

So, if you want to put something on a bucket list, make it
that.

We only have this incredibly short span of our lives to tell
our friends, family, and the generation of souls alive on earth
right now about Jesus. As the late Keith Green (hippie-turned-
Christian-songwriter) used to say, "This generation of Christians
is responsible for this generation of souls, all over the world."[4] We
are their only chance to hear.

The Party Crasher

Moses was not only the Abraham Lincoln and Billy Graham
of his generation, he was also its Lecrae. Bet you didn't know
that. Thankfully, a couple of his spoken-word pieces are recorded
for us in our Bibles.

My favorite is "Psalm 90," which is his meditation on God's
purpose for our lives. He explains to Israel that they will only

gain true wisdom by living with an awareness of the brevity of life. He prays:

> Teach us to number our days carefully so
> that we may develop wisdom in our hearts.
> (Ps. 90:12)

I love how Martin Luther translated this verse: "Teach us to reflect on the fact that we must die, so that we become wise."[5]

Thinking about the reality of death helps us gain the right perspective on life. We all understand, of course, in a propositional sense, that we are going to die. But understanding that cognitively and living in a conscious awareness of it are not the same thing.

The original lie that Satan whispered to Adam and Eve was, "You will not surely die." He tried to blind her to the reality of death. It's still what he whispers in our subconscious today. Even when we know, propositionally, that we are going to die, he convinces us to live oblivious to how close the reality of death is, and how permanent eternity will be.

The seventeenth-century French philosopher Blaise Pascal had a great analogy for this. He describes our lives like a giant party, full of happy people, loud music, and dancing, during which a monster unexpectedly bursts through the doors, grabs a random party-goer, mauls them in front of everyone, and drags their bloody corpse out of the room. Everyone watches in horror, and after it is over stares at each other in stunned silence for a few moments.

But then the band kicks back up and everyone returns to their frivolity, putting the horrendous display out of their minds. This horror is repeated every few moments until it becomes apparent that the monster is eventually coming for everyone in the room. Yet still the party goes on.

That monster, Pascal said, is our impending death. And our preferred way of dealing with it is *distraction*.

Turn up the music.

Our society, of course, has now elevated the art of distraction to epic levels. TVs are on everywhere. Auto-play on Netflix tries to get me to watch one episode of *The Office* after another until I have burned through all nine seasons. Your phone is probably alerting you to at least ten things happening right now that "need" your immediate attention. Social media apps like Instagram, Twitter, and TikTok are literally built on a psychology of addiction, created to keep you scrolling, swiping, scrolling, swiping. Trevor Haynes, writing for Harvard's *Science in the News*, shows how social media app developers make big bucks on your addiction: "By using algorithms to leverage our dopamine-driven reward circuitry, they stack the cards—and our brains—against us."[6]

In other words, there are some really smart people getting rich by fostering your addiction to . . . distraction. Our enemy has turned his Genesis 3 deception strategy into a high-tech Silicon Valley industry.

Go ahead, check your alerts.

I'll wait.

And still, the monster comes.

By the way, in the time it took you to read Pascal's example of the dance, the "monster" came for 105 people.[7]

How crazy, then, for us to never think about death? Historians estimate that about 106 billion people have lived on earth throughout its history. Only 7.7 billion people are alive right now. That means that for 95 percent of the people ever born, eternity is their only reality!

I remember my Sunday school teacher using an illustration that really drove this home, one that—though a little wacky—I've never forgotten. He said, "If a bird were to pick up a grain of sand in its beak and fly to Pluto with it, it would take him 26,655 years and three months to get there. If he dropped it off and then flew back to earth, picked up another grain of sand, and flew back, and did this until he had removed every grain of sand off of every beach in the world, that would be the first day of eternity."

No wonder James in the New Testament said our life is like the vapor our breath creates on a cold morning (James 4:14). It appears for just a moment, and then it's gone.

Only when we see the brevity of life—not only *see* it but *feel* it in our bones and marrow—will the rest of our lives come into focus.

Only when we live cognizant of death will we think wisely about life.

Make the Most of Your Mist

Jesus *constantly* pushed his hearers to reflect on the imminence of eternity. It was one of his most frequently repeated themes. In Luke 12 he told a story about a man who, because of his wild successes, lived without any thought of death. He amassed a fortune that guaranteed he and his descendants could weather any storm and ensured they would be comfortable for generations to come. In fact, on the day that he died, he'd just received news that another strategic business venture had paid off handsomely. Life was good.

"You fool!" That's what God said to him as he laid down his head to sleep that night.

> "This very night your life is demanded of you.
> And the things you have prepared—whose will
> they be?" (Luke 12:20)

What strikes me when I read this is that no overly immoral behavior was attributed to this man. He doesn't cheat, steal, sleep around, or extort the poor. God calls him a fool for only *one* reason: he lived as if life on earth was all there was.

> "That's how it is with the one who stores up
> treasure for himself and is not rich toward
> God." (Luke 12:21)

In Luke 16, Jesus told a parable that made this same point in perhaps an even more shocking way. Let me retell it in my own words:

> There was once an accounts manager for a really
> rich guy who, on Monday, was given his ter-
> mination notice. Friday would be his last day.

In despair, he went home and said to his wife, *"What am I going to do? I'm too old to start a new career, and I've grown accustomed to buying $5 Starbucks lattes every day and sitting in first class and there is no way I'm going back to Maxwell House and flying coach."*

But as he was saying these things, he had a brilliant idea. He called up several of his boss's clients and said something to each of them along the lines of:

"I see here that you owe my boss $100,000. I tell you what. If you'll pay $25,000 right now, I'll give you an official 'debt settled' certificate, and we'll just call it even." (You see, in those days account managers had full powers of attorney, and this guy still had that power, since technically he hadn't been fired yet, he'd only gotten his notice.)

Each debtor was, of course, shocked and pleased with the new arrangement. As they signed the paper, the manager winked at each and said, "Hey, later, just remember who took care of you."

(By the way, if you feel like this story is a little familiar, you might be thinking of *The Godfather.* The similarities are actually a little unnerving.)

And then, in what was surely a surprise ending for everyone listening, Jesus exclaimed,

> "What a wise manager! He used an opportunity he knew was coming to an end to prepare for the future, to make friends for his new future. That's how you should be with your money in regards to eternity."

According to Jesus, the immoral manager, though devious and shrewd, demonstrated simple, common-sense wisdom. Since he knew his time in his current position was short, he leveraged what he had to prepare for the next one. Such wisdom, Jesus lamented, is often lacking in the church:

> "And so I tell you, you likewise should use your money to make friends in eternity, so that when this life fails these friends may receive you into eternal dwellings." (Luke 16:9, my paraphrase)

If you *know* that your current reality is coming to an end, isn't it wise to use whatever few moments you have left in it to prepare for the next one?

In the same way, New Testament writers constantly pushed readers to consider the imminence of eternity. James warns, "Look, the judge stands at the door!" (James 5:9).

Paul concurs:

> The Lord is at hand. (Phil. 4:5 esv)

And,

> For you yourselves know very well that the day
> of the Lord will come just like a thief in the
> night. . . . So then, let us not sleep, like the rest,
> but let us stay awake and be self-controlled.
> (1 Thess. 5:2, 6)

Only an awareness of the imminence of eternity, Paul explains, can enable you to escape the seduction of materialism, creature comforts, bucket lists, and seashells. The nearness of eternity makes us realize that only two things *really* matter in life: the glory of God and the souls of people.

Gaining the Whole World and Losing Your Pinky

Jesus constantly stressed the common-sense nature of this approach to life. He once asked his listeners:

> "For what will it benefit someone if he gains the
> whole world yet loses his life? Or what will any-
> one give in exchange for his life?" (Matt. 16:26)

When I try to illustrate this point to teenagers, I ask: "How many of you, if I offered you $100 million in cold, hard cash to let me cut off your pinky, would take that deal?" Usually 99 percent of hands go up.

I then say, "Okay, what if it's not just your pinky, but I require your left arm up to your elbow?" A few less hands.

"Not just up your arm to your elbow but all the way up to your shoulder?" Fewer still.

Finally, I say, "Okay, not just your left arm but both arms, both legs, poke out your eyes, cut out your tongue and stop up your ears?"

No hands.

Except for one ninth-grade boy near the back. There's always one.

But for those with fully-developed frontal lobes, they reason, "What good is $100 million if I don't have any faculties with which to enjoy it? What kind of existence is that?"

This is exactly what Jesus is saying. Why is it, then, that so many are willing to give up far, far more to gain far, far less?

To trade the cause of Christ for material comforts is to sacrifice the eternal on the altar of the temporary.

> *Only one life, 'twill soon be past; only what's done*
> *for Christ will last.*

When the inevitable moment of your transition into eternity comes, are you going to enter rich toward God, or completely impoverished because you were so focused on checking off your bucket list?

Kick Your Bucket List

The bottom line? Kick your bucket list. Stop living as if the mist is going to last forever. Stop building sand castles that won't survive the evening tide.

What you do in life doesn't have to be meaningless. Your days have the potential to echo throughout eternity.

When I was a senior in college, I had agreed to meet my mother at a restaurant off of Highway 401 in Garner, North Carolina. I dreaded the conversation I was about to have with her. I sensed that God was calling me to forsake my law studies and serve overseas as a missionary.

My mom and dad were both Christians, but I just *knew* they would be disappointed. A lot of Christians support missions as a concept, but feel differently when it is their own kid going. My parents had sacrificed so much to get me into a good school and help me start out in life on a firm financial footing. I felt for sure they would think I was wasting my life.

I stumbled over my words. I wanted to convince my mom that God had genuinely called me. She listened silently.

Finally, I just said, "Mom, I know this is probably really disappointing for you. I know you must have had this vision of me staying close, making a comfortable living, and raising your grandkids in a place where you could see them every day. But I don't think that's what God has for me."

And then I just sat there.

I was ready for the argument. Objections like, "We've invested too much just to let you throw it all away." Maybe tears. But instead, she said: "J. D., your father and I have been praying for God's will for you your entire life. And if this is how God wants to use your life, we won't stand in your way. In fact, there's nothing that would make us prouder than knowing you gave your life back to God for his service. If God wants to use the gifts he gave you on an international mission field, we'll support you all the way."

I was stunned. But she wasn't done.

"We'll have all eternity to enjoy the blessings of our family . . . and so, if we miss out on some of them down here, that's okay. But we've only got a few years to ensure that people's sons and daughters around the world have a chance to be included in our forever family."

That's an eternal perspective.

In the spring of 1951, prospective missionary Jim Elliot wrote a letter to his parents before leaving for Ecuador, trying to convince his parents of the same thing. Here's what he said:

> I do not wonder that you were saddened at the word of my going to South America . . . This is nothing else than what the Lord Jesus warned us of when He told the disciples that they must become so infatuated with the kingdom and following Him that all other allegiances must become as though they were not. And He never excluded the family tie.
>
> In fact, those loves which we regard as closest, He told us must become as hate in comparison with our desires to uphold His cause. Grieve not, then, if your sons seem to desert you, but rejoice, rather, seeing the will of God done gladly. Remember how the Psalmist described children? He said that they were as

an heritage from the Lord, and that every man
should be happy who had his quiver full of
them. And what is a quiver full of but arrows?
And what are arrows for but to shoot? So, with
the strong arms of prayer, draw the bowstring
back and let the arrows fly—all of them,
straight at the Enemy's hosts.

"Give of thy sons to bear the message glorious,
Give of thy wealth to speed them on their way,
Pour out thy soul for them in prayer victorious,
And all thou spendest Jesus will repay."[8]

Jim never made it back. He, his wife Elisabeth, and their
parents are now in eternity together. What do you think they
would tell us?

Worth it, or not?

"Letting the arrows fly" is a powerful metaphor not just for
parents to think of with regard to their children but for all of us
to think about with regard to our lives. God gave us whatever he
gave us to launch out for the mission. Arrows are made to shoot
toward the enemy, not sit idly in a quiver.

Only one life to live, 'twill soon be past. Only
what's done for Christ will last.

Truly, he is no fool who gives what he cannot keep to gain
what he cannot lose.

Chapter 3

The Myth of Calling

"'Not called!' did you say? 'Not heard the call,' I think
you should say. Put your ear down to the Bible, and hear
Him bid you go and pull sinners out of the fire of sin.
Put your ear down to the burdened, agonized heart of
humanity, and listen to its pitiful wail for help . . . Then
look Christ in the face—whose mercy you have professed
to obey—and tell Him whether you will join . . . [Him]
in the march to publish His mercy to the world."
—WILLIAM BOOTH, FOUNDER OF THE SALVATION ARMY

One sunny Sunday October morning two cars pulled into our church parking lot and five college students piled out. They parked in the fire lane. They sat on the third row from the back and slipped out right after the service. But they must have enjoyed themselves because the next weekend five hundred of them showed up.

Piling out of the same two cars, by the way.

Students bring a lot of great things to church—enthusiasm, optimism, evangelistic zeal—but money is not one of them. Our average weekly attendance in that season basically doubled, while average weekly giving went up only about $2.00.

One of my favorite memories of that season is of an usher coming to me between services with an offering bucket, and in it a bacon, egg, and cheese biscuit from McDonald's, from a college student. With a little note on it that read, "Silver and gold have I none, but such as I have, give I unto you."

But as the population of students at our weekend services began to swell, our leadership realized something about our future: while we might never be the wealthiest church, we would have a large pool of potential missionaries, a huge swath of people who wanted their lives to count and were eager to hear what God had to say.

We have put in front of them a vision that many find revolutionary—though it is arguably the most basic component of Christian discipleship. It is this:

> *Every follower of Jesus is called to leverage his or*
> *her life for the Great Commission.*

One of the most destructive myths alive in the church today, I believe, is that only a few are called to the ministry.

Cheerios, Burning Bushes, and the Call of God

Many Christians believe that "calling" is a sacred experience reserved for a select few conferred through a mystical manifestation. They assume that if God wants something significant from their lives, he'll communicate it through some kind of burning bush, wet-fleece/dry-fleece dramatic sign. I call this the "Cheerios" method of discerning the will of God. If God has something significant for you, he'll spell it out in your Cheerios. The little o's will mysteriously form, "go to Nepal" or "be a pastor" or whatever.

But here's the truth: *All Christians are called to ministry.* Not necessarily to *vocational* ministry but to leverage their lives for the Great Commission.

That call, you see, was included in the initial call to follow Jesus. "Follow me," Jesus said, "and I will make you fish for people" (Matt. 4:19). That means when you accepted Jesus, you accepted the call to mission.

As I said in chapter 1, the question is no longer *if* you are called, only where and how.

To be fair, I have friends who point to a dramatic moment God used to call them into vocational ministry. It is also true that the Spirit of God will plant in the hearts of some a desire for vocational ministry—a desire to lead a church or devote their energies full-time into evangelistic mission. That desire, Paul says, is a good thing, and often the way God calls people into vocational ministry (1 Tim. 3:1). God put on Nehemiah's heart, for example, an insatiable yearning to rebuild the walls of Jerusalem, and Nehemiah correctly interpreted those desires as the call of God (Neh. 2:12).

But in the most basic sense, all Christians are called to the mission. All Christians are called to leverage their lives for the

Great Commission. That's what Jesus called you to when he called you to follow him.

That means you need to think about the mission of God when you choose where and how to pursue your career. *You have to get a job somewhere, so why not get a job in a place where God is doing something strategic?* Lots of factors go into where you pursue your career—where you can make the best money, where family lives, cool places to live, etc. And these are all well and good. But why shouldn't the kingdom of God be the *largest* of those factors? Isn't that what it means to be a follower of Jesus? To seek *first* God's kingdom in all that you do?

Lot, Abraham's nephew, chose his career primarily based on money. It did not turn out well for Lot. Particularly Lot's wife— things got pretty salty for her.[1] It will not turn out well for you either if you make money the largest factor in where and how you pursue your career.

Here's how I'd summarize pursuing the will of God in your career: *whatever you're good at, do it well to the glory of God, and do it somewhere strategic for the mission of God.*

God didn't make everyone good at preaching or pastoring, but he made you good at something—that might be architecture, education, law, medicine, business, or any number of other things. Whatever it is, do it well for the glory of God. But also do it somewhere strategic for the mission of God.

Sure, God sometimes instructs people to walk away from their careers and pursue ministry, like he did with Peter (Luke 5:1–11). But more often than not he uses people *in* their careers. As the book of Acts indicates, God gave us our careers, in part, to be vehicles of gospel proclamation and gospel demonstration. For some, God calls them to leave their careers for the mission, for others, to *leverage* them. But either way, we're all called to the mission.

How can we say we take the gospel seriously and not make its advance a major factor in how we pursue our careers?

Be the *Them*

From the time I was a child, the miracle of Jesus that probably most captivated my imagination was his feeding of the five thousand. With only five loaves and two fish, something like a Hebrew Happy Meal, Jesus fed more than five thousand hungry men. There are multiple things we can learn about ministry from that miracle, but one of the most important is this: *God has already placed in the hands of his church everything necessary to complete the Great Commission.*

Just as the little boy had only to open up his hands and offer up his five loaves and two fish, so have we only to offer up our lives into his hands to see the lost multitudes fed to abundance.

The book of Acts demonstrates this over and over. God uses ordinary people as the tip of the gospel spear. Throughout the book of Acts ordinary people outpace even the apostles in gospel expansion.

The first time the gospel leaves the borders of Jerusalem, it is not in the mouths of the apostles, but ordinary people. Jesus had clearly told his disciples that he wanted his gospel preached in Jerusalem, Judea, Samaria, and the uttermost parts of the earth.

But by Acts 7, the gospel seems "stuck" in Jerusalem. The first seven chapters of Acts contain *not one* story of anyone leaving Jerusalem with the gospel.

That all changes with the story of Stephen. Stephen, an "ordinary" believer (not an apostle), provides such humble, sacrificial service to widows in his community that he is brought before the Sanhedrin to explain what he's doing.

His bold testimony to Christ starts a riot, and believers are driven out of Jerusalem into Judea and Samaria. As they go, they carry the gospel with them (Acts 8:4). Luke (the writer of Acts), goes out of his way to point out that, of those who left preaching the word, not a single apostle was involved:

> . . . and all *except the apostles* were scattered
> throughout the land of Judea and Samaria . . .
> [and] those who were scattered went on their
> way preaching the word. (Acts 8:1, 4, emphasis
> mine)

God accomplished through the preaching of a layman what the apostles had been unable to do in seven chapters.

Later in that same chapter, we see the first "international mission trip" taken by Philip, another one of those laymen. The Spirit of God guides him to a desert road junction where he meets an Ethiopian government official whom he leads to Christ and baptizes (Acts 8:26–40).

According to the church father Irenaeus, this "Ethiopian eunuch" returned to sub-Saharan Africa as its first gospel emissary.[2]

One layman, Philip, obedient to the Spirit, was able to get the gospel farther around the world than had all the apostles up to that point.

This pattern of "anonymous" Christians spreading the gospel continues throughout Acts. As Stephen Neill notes in his classic *History of Christian Missions*:

> Nothing is more notable than the anonymity of these early missionaries. . . . Luke does not turn aside to mention the name of a single one of those pioneers who laid the foundation. Few, if any, of the great Churches were really founded by apostles. Peter and Paul may have *organized* the Church in Rome. They certainly did not found it.[3]

Dr. Neill points to the existence of three primary Christian "centers" by the end of the first century: Antioch, Alexandria, and Rome. The most remarkable thing about those centers, he says, is that we have no idea who brought the movement to them, or who planted their first churches.

The church at Antioch, for example, which served as the hub for missionary activity for the last half of the book of Acts, was planted by those scattered there after Stephen's sermon (Acts 11:19). Here's what's significant: Luke uses no personal names in reporting the account of those who established the most strategic church planting center in the ancient world. He only says that the Lord's hand "was with *them*" (Acts 11:21, emphasis mine).

"Them."

As my friend Vance Pitman says, that is Luke's way of saying, "a bunch of dudes whose names I won't mention because you wouldn't recognize them and won't hear anything about them again anyway." They are the kinds of people who get listed in the credits of the movie as "Bystander #3."

It was Apollos, a layman, another "them," who first carried the gospel into Ephesus. And yet another group of "them" first established the church at Rome. These believers hadn't traveled to Rome on a formal mission trip, they were carried there through the normal relocations that come with business and life! But as they went, they made disciples and established churches (Acts 8:5–8; 18:24–19:1; 28:15).

Thank God for *them*.

Throughout Christian history, the gospel has nearly always spread—and *stuck*—because ordinary people like you carried the gospel wherever they went. Ordinary people are the tip of the gospel spear.

Again, the question is no longer if you are called to leverage your life for the Great Commission, only where and how. However God gifted you, he gifted you with the Great Commission in mind.

Maybe nobody in Christianity knows your name, but you can be part of the most powerful and effective mission force ever established—"Team *THEM*."

Increasing the Mission Force by 600 Percent

What if I told you that the pieces were already in place to increase the missionary force in the unreached world by 600 percent?

Currently, there are 40,000 evangelical missionaries (from all denominations) living in what missiologists call the 10/40 window. (That's the area of the world located between the 10-degree and 40-degree latitude lines, where the most unreached people groups live.) Praise God for those missionaries, but that's a pretty tiny number when you stack it up against the hundreds of millions of people there who don't know Jesus.

But also, right now, two *million* Americans work in (so-called) "secular" employment in that same 10/40 window. About half of them identify as Christians. Even if you write off 90 percent of that number as representing people not really serious about their faith, that still leaves *200,000* who take their commitment to Christ seriously. That's 200,000 of the *THEM*.

Imagine if every one of them recognized that their primary identity in life was a "disciple-making-disciple," responsible to leverage whatever opportunities they have for gospel impact.

That would raise the number of "missionaries" from 40,000 to *240,000* without costing the church another dime. (And that's only counting American Christians!)

Right after my dad retired from the textile company where he had worked for almost forty years, his company asked him to come back to oversee the development of some new factories in the 10/40 window. There he rubbed shoulders with Asian businessmen that our mission teams could never get close to on a mission trip doing "English corners" and passing out water bottles. He was instrumental in seeing a couple of them come to faith in Christ, and part of helping to establish a new church there. The local business community discovered that my mom was a professor, and they asked her if she would teach a class on English literature. My mom responded that literature was not her field, but they said it didn't matter. She asked if she could teach from the Bible and they said, "Yes, that would be wonderful." She taught a class in which some of this region's best and brightest received a book they'd only heard about and their first instruction in it.

Total cost to the church: $0.00.

In fact, we made money on the deal because he kept sending his tithe back the whole time he was there.

Many of you, if you look into your hands, might discover that you're already holding the key God has given for the unlocking of the nations.

It appears that God has arranged even the current economic topography of our world as an opportunity for mission. Missiologist Mike Barnett notes:

> Twenty percent of the world's population lives in Muslim countries, yet only 4 percent of world trade comes from these countries. . . . We are living at a point in world history of unprecedented opportunities for the expansion of the Christian faith. No country is

closed to business. In no country is it illegal to
love people. There are huge doors of opportunity wide open before us, if we are willing to
equip ourselves adequately and walk through
them. Countries considered "closed" to missionaries welcome Christians who come as
[businesspeople].[4]

For business leaders, that 10/40 window isn't a "window" at
all. It's a wide-open open door.

Of course, maybe the place God will direct you to invest your
life is right in your hometown. And if that's where he's called you,
that's exactly where you need to be. But the point is that all of us
are to live *sent* somewhere, and living *sent* implies that you have
asked God where he wants to use you in the mission.

Not all Christians go overseas, but all live sent.

Get Good at Your Job

The book of Proverbs says, "Do you see a person skilled in
his work? He will stand in the presence of kings" (Prov. 22:29).
If you are good at your job, even kings will be interested in what
you have to offer.

My friend Mike is head of neurology at one of our nation's
most prestigious medical schools. A few times a year his university sends him to remote parts of Asia, right in the middle of
some of the least reached places on the planet. There he gives

lectures to their medical professionals and government workers and mentors their medical students.

The university he serves at is not a Christian one, and the places he goes are often closed to Christianity. But he said to me recently, "Because of the success God has given me, I can pretty much say whatever I want in these forums. So, I always give my testimony and explain how the gospel shapes my approach to medicine."

Another friend, Henry, is one of North Carolina's most successful entrepreneurs. He gets invited all over the world to instruct and inspire others. He uses that opportunity to explain how his faith shapes his attitude toward work, and he leverages his investments to empower businesses that are led by Christians committed to the Great Commission.

Or consider the story of Louise Celia Fleming, the first African American female missionary. Fleming was born a slave, but after the Civil War, she went to school to become a teacher. She taught in St. Augustine, Florida, for a while, until an 1880 visit to Brooklyn. In Brooklyn, Fleming met a minister who was so impressed by her knowledge of Scripture that he encouraged her to apply to Shaw University in North Carolina.

Fleming applied. She was accepted. And a few short years later, she graduated from Shaw as the class valedictorian.

One year after graduation, she received a request from the Women's Baptist Foreign Missionary Society to be their first teacher in the Congo. Fleming accepted, becoming the first black woman appointed to serve as a missionary-teacher. She used her position to platform and send scores of Congolese students to college—usually to her very own Shaw University.

Be the best you can possibly be at your career. Get good at it. Your skills might very well be the thing God uses to place you before kings. And when you are there, tell them about Jesus. Slogging your way through law school or grinding through a grueling internship may not feel godly, but it might be the very thing God uses to put you in a place where people have no choice but to listen to you. Few things adorn the gospel as much as a fervent work ethic.

Maybe These Are the Good Ol' Days

We are poised today for a gospel expansion as great as anything ever experienced in Christian history.

In the final episode of *The Office,* character Andy Bernard says something I've always thought profound. As the characters begin to realize their nine years together in "the office" are coming to a close, Andy turns to the camera and says, "I wish there was a way to know you're in 'the good old days' before you've actually left them."

Pay attention in church, and you'll hear Christian leaders talk about the "good ol' days" of the church when Peter and Paul preached with breathtaking boldness. Small groups prayed all night. Martyrs cheerfully sacrificed their lives. Peter's hankies healed people, and impostors got struck dead during the offering. Drowsy people who dozed during sermons fell out of windows and died, only to be resurrected by the long-winded preachers who put them to sleep. The church was an unstoppable movement.

The only problem, historian Rodney Stark notes, is that if you had been alive during this period, most of the time it wouldn't have *felt* like you were part of an unstoppable movement. Here's why I say that: the best demographic estimates point to a grand total of only 7,500 believers worldwide at the end of the first century.[5] We imagine Peter and Paul conducting huge, Billy-Graham-style evangelistic rallies with thousands of conversions daily. Not exactly.

The growth of Christianity was numerically rather unimpressive throughout that first century. In fact, Origen (b. AD 184– d. AD 254) described the Christian movement in his day as still a few scattered communities, geographically broad but numerically insignificant.[6] At his death, they still amounted to less than 2 percent of the Roman Empire's population!

Yet, by AD 312, Christians had become so numerous that the emperor, Constantine, decided to convert to Christianity *for political reasons.* Over half of the Roman Empire now identified as Christian!

What happened between the end of the first century and AD 312? What made this group of scattered and politically insignificant believers so numerous that the most powerful man in the world had to take note?

Rodney Stark attributes it to the power of multiplication.[7]

Remember this annoying math riddle from middle school?

> If you have a choice between receiving $10,000
> a day for thirty days, or getting $0.01 doubled
> each day, which would you choose?

I was like most middle school students. I chose the $10K daily without skipping a beat. I mean, think about it. How much could one do with $10,000? In thirty days, I'd have $300,000. How could someone even spend that much money? After getting an Atari—shoot, *ten* Ataris—a brand new, enormous, *32-inch* technicolor TV, and the fanciest car on the market—a 1982 DeLorean, just like Marty McFly—I'd still have $200,000 left.

But then my math teacher explained that I should have started with the penny. Sure, after the first week, I'd only have a couple of bucks, but by the end of the month, I'd have $10,737,418.23. That's a whole fleet of DeLoreans!

That's the power of multiplication. You see, the early church had very little compared to what we have today: no grand auditoriums. No publishing presses, book contracts, TV stations, or political power. No Religious Freedom Restoration Acts. Virtually no money.

What they did have, though, was an ingrained understanding that each Christian was called to multiply and that God himself was in them empowering them to do it. *Every* disciple was expected, therefore, to make disciples. Every new church was planted with the expectation that it would reproduce.

And that produced a greater worldwide impact than we do today with all of our stuff.

Albert Einstein was reportedly once asked, "What is the most powerful force in the universe?" His reply? "Compound interest." So it is with churches. The power of multiplication far exceeds the impact of great preaching, professional worship bands, and impressive facilities.

Over the last one hundred years, we've witnessed the building of some of the largest, most impressive megachurches in Christian history. We've seen Billy Graham gather crowds of epic proportions. These things were awesome, and we need more of them. And yet, despite all this, the percentage of people going to church each weekend in America has *gone down*.

The early church had none of what we have, yet was able to do what we haven't been able to do!

What if God was using our missional frustration to call us back to our New Testament roots? What if the current obstacles we face in the church—like funding shortages, a decline in political influence, and increasing cultural opposition—were designed by God to return us to the one thing that has propelled the church forward in every generation?

Today, there are more Southern Baptist *churches* in the United States—just Southern Baptist—than either Starbucks, Subway, or McDonald's.

> What if each of these churches committed themselves to multiplying?
>
> What if they began to measure their success by sending capacity rather than seating capacity?

What if each believer saw the Great Commission
          as *their* responsibility?

Might not our great-grandchildren look back on this time
period and see these as "the good ol' days"?

This will only happen when ordinary believers see themselves as *called* to ministry.

Francis Chan said it well:

> Long gone are the days when [we should be]
> content with a bunch of people who sing out
> loud, don't divorce, and give to missions. I now
> want to know I can drop off any member of my
> church in a city and that person could grow in
> Jesus, make disciples, and help start a church.[8]

It starts with you. God has called you to multiply. To bring
forth fruit that will abide for eternity (John 15:16).

That sounds daunting, I know. But, as Jesus explains, it's not
something you have to do on your own. It's something he does
through you when you put your "yes" on the table.

It's not about you for him, it's about him in you.

Chapter 4

Greater Than John

> "Not everything that comes from heaven
> has your name on it. But something does.
> Figure out what that is, and get after it."
> —LARRY OSBORNE

It's time for a little Bible trivia! Grab your pen and pad. Judges in the back, start the clock. Somebody ask Alexa to play the *Jeopardy!* theme.

Q: Who was Jesus' favorite preacher?

Tick, tick, tick.

Ten more seconds.

Hint: Rhymes with "on the Baptist."

That's right! *John the Baptist.*

Jesus loved the preaching of John the Baptist. He said,

> "Truly I tell you, among those born of women
> [that's all of us, by the way] no one greater than
> John the Baptist has appeared." (Matt. 11:11a)

Jesus was always up-to-date on John's podcast, "Fire, Brimstone, and Ill-Fitting Clothes." He wore a little bracelet that said, "WWJTBD?" and always came to John's defense when John was featured on *Preachers 'N' Sneakers*. When John walked in the room, Jesus would join in with the rest of John's fans who would put their fists up and chant, "JTB! JTB!"

Okay, maybe not all that. But clearly he was a big fan of John's preaching. Which makes what he said next all the more remarkable:

> ". . . but the least in the kingdom of heaven is
> greater than he." (Matt. 11:11b)

The *least* in his kingdom is greater than John, the greatest of all the prophets? What exactly does "least in the kingdom of heaven" mean?

It means you have the least, personally, to offer the kingdom. You know the least about the Bible; you have the fewest spiritual gifts; you show the least leadership potential. Stuff like that.

Someone reading this book right now is the "least in the kingdom of heaven" of that group. I'm not trying to be mean, but statistically that *has to be* true. Somebody has to be at the bottom.

Maybe you're saying to yourself right now, *Hey! I think it might be me?* And maybe God in heaven is nodding his head right now saying, "Yep. It's you. You're at the bottom of the pile." Someone anonymously sent me an award this year for "Worst Christian Influencer of 2019." So, maybe it's me! Yet, to whomever it is, Jesus says in this verse, "*You*—Mr. Bottom-of-the-Pile—you have more potential in ministry than even John the Baptist."

You see, you and I have something ol' JTB never had. A couple of things, actually. First, we know the fullness of the gospel, of which John, as an Old Testament prophet, only knew a part.[1] Second, we know the fullness of the Spirit, whose presence John and the other Old Testament prophets only knew a portion of. (John had the Holy Spirit in one sense, but you and I have received him as the permanent endowment of adopted sons and daughters of God.)

And if that's true, it changes our understanding of ministry. Because the Holy Spirit is in us, power in ministry is no longer about what we do for him, but what he does through us. It's no longer about our *ability* in ministry but our *availability* to the Spirit.

Scripture shows us that God can do more with one willing vessel submitted to the Spirit than all the talent man can muster.

Don't believe me? Well, I didn't say it first.

The Spirit Inside Us Is Better Than Jesus Beside Us?

The promises Jesus made about the Holy Spirit's potential in believers are so extraordinary that we tend not to take them seriously. For example, he promised his disciples:

> "Truly I tell you, the one who believes in me
> will also do the works that I do. And he will
> do even greater works than these, because I am
> going to the Father." (John 14:12)

Umm, excuse me . . . GREATER works than Jesus? Do you know anyone who's ever done a *greater* work than raising the dead, walking on water, or calming the seas?

Even if you disregard the miracles, have any of us ever preached a greater sermon than the Sermon on the Mount? Anyone ever counseled someone with greater insight than Jesus counseled the woman at the well? Anyone ever pray with greater insight into the purposes of God than Jesus demonstrates in John 17?

Can anything any of us have ever done be regarded as "greater" than what Jesus did?

Yet Jesus promised our works would be greater than his. How so?

They are not greater in their *quality* but in their quantity. The same power that brought Jesus back from the dead is at work in each of his followers today, and the potential impact of an entire body of believers submitted to the Spirit is greater than if Jesus himself had stayed behind to lead the mission.[2] If you had to choose between having Jesus himself as your pastor or a church full of Spirit-filled believers, if you understood the power of the Spirit, you'd choose that option every time.

Jesus even told his disciples,

"It is *for your benefit* that I go away, because
if I don't go away the Counselor will not
come to you. If I go, I will send him to you."
(John 16:7, emphasis mine)

Again, how absurd must that have sounded to those first
disciples? It was to their *benefit* that Jesus leave them and return
to heaven?

What would it have been like to walk around with Jesus for
three years? You're late to work, so BAM! Jesus parts the cars in
front of you like the Red Sea, and you drive to work on an open
highway. You forget your lunch, so Jesus takes a saltine from the
break room, and BAM! multiplies it into a feast for the whole
office with twelve baskets of leftovers. Your dog dies, and BAM!
he raises it back to life. Your cat dies . . .

BAM! He grabs a shovel and helps you bury it.

Okay, again—maybe not all that. But obviously it would
come with some major advantages, right? Yet Jesus promised that
something about the Spirit's power in us would be more advanta-
geous than Jesus remaining bodily on earth with us.

Sincere question: Does your experience with the Spirit match
the magnitude of that promise?

Jesus said that if we *really* understood the power and potential of the Spirit in ordinary believers, if we had a choice between
having Jesus *beside* us and the Spirit *inside* us, we would choose
the Spirit every time.

That's the extent to which God promises to use us in his
mission.

If that's true, how might it change what you are planning to do with your life?

God Does His Greatest Work through Simple Acts of Obedience

God can accomplish more through one simple act of obedience than the most talented leaders can accomplish in a lifetime on their own.

As we saw in the last chapter, God accomplished more in global evangelism through the obedience of one layman, Stephen, than all the apostles had been able to accomplish in the seven chapters of Acts leading up to that point. That kind of power for impact is still available today.

When I was in college, I was the leader of a small campus ministry. By small, I mean that there weren't more than ten of us in the whole thing. We decided we wanted to host a big evangelistic event on campus. We booked the largest auditorium on campus and did all the usual promo—booked a local worship band, passed out fliers promising free hot dogs, etc.

The day before the event, I had that huge knot in my stomach that always comes on the eve of massive, humiliating failure. (I've had enough failures in my life to know exactly what it feels like when one is moments away. It's like the ache in his bones my granddad used to get before a big rain.) Our leadership team was sitting in the school cafeteria working through the final details of our event. I was bracing myself and our team for the worst when I heard a small commotion coming from just over my left shoulder. I turned, and there on top of the table stood one of the girls on our leadership team. She was small, quiet, and shy. But there she stood, stamping her foot and calling for the attention of all four to five hundred people in the lunchroom. Yes, it was as awkward as you are imagining it.

"I'm sorry to interrupt your lunch," she said, "but I wanted to invite all of you to an event we're hosting tomorrow night in the campus theatre. One of our friends is going to share his story about how he came to know Jesus and tell you how Jesus can change your life, too. And we really want you all to be there because Jesus is the greatest thing in our lives. Please come." And then she started to sit back down.

"Oh, and there will be free hot dogs," she added.

We all stared at her.

She quietly resumed her lunch.

"Uh, what was *that*?" I asked, glancing into her glass to see if someone had added in a little something interesting to her Diet Coke.

"I'm not sure," she said, "I just felt like the Spirit of God wanted me to do that."

I'm not saying that obedience to the Spirit means you start standing up on tables in public dining facilities. On the whole, I'd counsel against it. But I will tell you that more than seven hundred people showed up the next night, and fifty-one people made first-time professions of faith.

God does his greatest works through small acts of obedience from seemingly insignificant people.

Just last week I saw it happen at our church through a guy named "Derrick." Derrick got saved through the prison ministry at our church, and after being released from prison, he joined that ministry as part of the leadership team, going back into the same prison he once was held in. He hasn't been able to get his license yet, so he takes a Lyft each week to church.

On the way to church, he shared his testimony with the driver. The driver said that he had grown up a Muslim, but had recently had a series of dreams in which he thought Jesus might be speaking to him. When they pulled into our church's parking lot, Derrick told him, "Listen—I think you need to come into church with me." He did, and that night, when I gave an invitation, he came forward to profess his faith in Christ and be baptized.

Because of the gift of the Holy Spirit, it's not about the abilities you bring to the table, but the willingness you lay on the table. God doesn't call the equipped; he equips the called. What makes you capable of extraordinary things is not extraordinary gifts, but an extraordinary willingness to be used by God.

As D. L. Moody used to say, "The world has yet to see what God can do through one man [or woman] fully submitted to him."

Maybe you're supposed to be "that one"?

Bible scholars have long noted that the book of Acts seems wrongly named. (It was Irenaeus who late in the second century first called it the "Acts of the Apostles.") If anything, it should probably be called the "Acts of the Holy Spirit," because it is not a record of the heroic efforts of a few super-Christians, but the record of the Holy Spirit's work through the faithful obedience of a bunch of ordinary Christians. It tells the stories of a bunch of people who can barely keep up with all that God wants to do through them.

If we want to experience the "greater things" Jesus promised like they did, we need to start listening to the Holy Spirit like they did too.

Does He Speak to You?

But perhaps you ask, "How do I know what he is leading me to do?"

That's a great question. The short answer is that you experience his leadership through a) his Word, b) the ministry yearnings he puts into your heart, c) revealed gifts, d) open doors, and e) the counsel of those in the church who can see what God is doing in your life. Pressing much further into each of these areas is beyond the scope of this book, but there are several good studies out there that can help you press in on those questions if you are interested.[3]

For now, I just want to make sure you understand that, if you're a Christian, the Spirit wants to use you extraordinarily in his kingdom.

Experiencing the Spirit's leadership is not a thing relegated to the past. The early church *depended* on it. They were desperate for it. The Holy Spirit appears fifty-nine times in the book of Acts, and in thirty-six of those instances he is speaking, leading believers to great effectiveness in his name.

I understand that Acts represents a unique period of apostolic history. But you can't convince me that the only narrative book given to us describing the ministry of the church is filled with stories of people whose experiences are to have nothing in common with our own. The early church was desperate for this leadership. Shouldn't we be, also?

As John Newton (the Puritan and hymnwriter of "Amazing Grace") said, "Is it really true that that which the early church so depended on—the leadership of the Spirit—is irrelevant to us today?"[4]

The future of the mission depends on our willingness to commune with that Spirit and listen to his directives.

Do you want your life to count for eternity? It starts with surrendering to the leading of the Holy Spirit and listening for his voice.

Not Everything That Comes from Heaven Has Your Name on It. But Something Does.

Without the leadership of the Spirit, we won't know what part of the mission belongs to us. The overwhelming vastness of the task has a way of crushing us. In the light of so much need, what possible difference could any of us make?

It is paralyzing for me to think of the *billions* of people in the world with little or no access to the gospel, or to think of the 2.5 billion people that live without adequate nourishment or consistent access to clean water. Or the 2 billion kids who live in poverty or the nearly 100,000 kids who die *every week* of preventable, hunger-related diseases.

Can I really make a significant impact?

The good news is that God did not make any of us responsible for the entire mission. Jesus bears that responsibility himself. He said,

> "*I* will build my church, and the gates of Hades
> will not overpower it." (Matt. 16:18, emphasis
> mine)

He's the master builder of the church, the sole owner of the mission.

God said to King David,

> "*Be still,* and know that I am God. I will be
> exalted among the nations." (Ps. 46:10 ESV,
> emphasis mine)

Salvation belongs to him. Our responsibility is only to yield ourselves to be used by him where he directs *us.*

Recently, I learned the denomination that does the best job mobilizing their people for mission was . . . the Pentecostals. Honestly, I was a little surprised. Because, after all, I'm a Baptist, and we Baptists feel like missions is *our thing.* I mean, we're the ones with the big mission boards, who collect yearly offerings named after mission heroes, and who boast many of the great missionary heroes of the past: William Carey, Adoniram Judson, Lottie Moon, Amy Carmichael, Billy Graham.

And yet, per capita, Pentecostals do a better job of raising up, empowering, and sending out their members. Why? Gary Tyra suggests that it is because Pentecostals emphasize Spirit empowerment while Baptists focus on world need.[5] World need is paralyzing; Spirit-gifting is uplifting. I may not be able to save the world, but I can obey the Spirit's direction for my life. Evidently, being gift-driven is more empowering than being guilt-driven!

Pastor Larry Osborne, a mentor and counselor to me, years ago spoke words that set me free: "J. D., not everything that comes from heaven has your name on it. But something does. Figure out what that is and get after it."

Have you figured out what has *your* name on it? Because only then will you begin to experience the fullness of the Spirit's power.

But there's something else you are going to have to believe, too, if you are going to follow the Holy Spirit with the abandon necessary to make an impact on eternity. It's called "the law of the harvest," and it's one of the most important principles of Christian living.

Chapter 5

The Law of the Harvest

"I have held many things in my hands, and I
have lost them all; but whatever I have placed
in God's hands, that I still possess."
—MARTIN LUTHER

armers in Oklahoma during the late 1930s faced an
excruciating choice.

Throughout the 1920s, rain had been plentiful and the harvests abundant, and many city workers had left factory jobs in the Northeast for the chance of a fortune in the great American Midwest. The stock market crash of 1929 motivated even more. But in 1931, the rains stopped. To make matters worse, sloppy farming techniques had destroyed the grasses that preserved moisture during times of drought. The dry ground caused massive dust storms, which destroyed the remaining fields. Fortunes were swept away in clouds of dull, gray dust. By the fall of 1939, thousands of farmers had returned empty-handed to the East.

Many who remained had just enough grain to feed themselves and their families for another year. They could sell the grain and move back home. Or they could plant it. If the rains came, their seed would gain a hundredfold harvest. If not, they'd be left with nothing.

Many planted, in faith—in hope—that rain would come.

And in the fall of 1939, it did.[1]

Life in the World Comes through Death in the Church

The law of the harvest states that you can only reap what first you sow. Planting involves risk. If the rains don't come, you are left with nothing. But if you never take the risk, you will never see the harvest.

Jesus turned to the law of the harvest to explain to his disciples the mentality necessary to reach the world with the gospel. A group of Gentiles had come seeking an audience with him (John 12:21). They had heard about this miracle-working, grace-preaching Savior from Nazareth, and they wanted to see him for themselves.

Note that this is a pivotal moment not just in John's Gospel, but in the Bible itself. The Gentiles, whom God had promised to one day bring into the blessings of the Messiah, are reaching out to Jesus. Jesus knows (even if his disciples haven't quite caught on yet) that this has been God's plan from the beginning of his rescue work on earth. And here they are.

This is a big moment.

Which makes Jesus' statement to his disciples all the more significant. He is telling his disciples what must be true about *them* if generations of Gentiles are to know about him:

> "The hour has come for the Son of Man to
> be glorified. Truly I tell you, unless a grain of
> wheat falls to the ground and dies, it remains by
> itself. But if it dies, it produces much fruit. The
> one who loves his life will lose it, and the one
> who hates his life in this world will keep it for
> eternal life." (John 12:23–25)

His use of the seed analogy might at first strike us as odd because I typically don't think of a seed planted into the dirt as *dying*. I think of it, in fact, as just beginning to live.

But in one sense it is dying. Its life as a seed is over. Its outer shell crumbles, and no longer can it be consumed as food. .

But from that seed's death comes the potential of new life. And not just a single life but life multiplied from generation to generation. Each seed might yield ten times, a hundred times, even *a thousand* times more than its original capacity. In the right conditions, it will replicate forever.

The same is true for the church. Life in the world comes only through death in the church. What you hang onto, you lose. What you give away, you keep for eternity.

Death Precedes Resurrection

The principle of death before life permeates Scripture. God often requires his followers to "die" to what is most precious to them before he will infuse it with divine life. God multiplied Abraham's offspring only *after* Abraham demonstrated that he was willing to sacrifice Isaac, his only son, on the altar.[2] He multiplied the oil and flour of the widow of Zarephath only *after* she offered the last of it to make Elijah, God's prophet, a meal (1 Kings 17:7–24). Jesus multiplied the little boy's five loaves and two fish to feed the multitudes only *after* the little boy put them in his hands (John 6:1–15). God endowed the staff of Moses with great power only *after* he threw it down in surrender (Exod. 4:3–4).

Whatever is most precious to you has to be offered up in sacrifice before God will endow it with power for the kingdom. Only what's planted can be harvested.

I learned this from one of the first biographies I read in college, the life story of Keith Green, the iconic hippie-turned-gospel songwriter who died tragically in a plane crash in 1982. Keith is regarded by many to be the most powerful Christian songwriter of his generation. He was saved in the great "Jesus movement" of the 1970s, and his music brought many to faith in Christ and inspired countless more to go to the mission field.[3]

Keith thought of his ministry as two distinct eras. He had always been a gifted musician, and in the early years of his faith he wrote many "helpful" Christian songs. But there came a point in his life where he felt God tell him that his music was too important to him, and that he should lay it down. He walked away from it, assuming he would never perform publicly again.

A year later, the Spirit of God directed him to pick his music back up. Now it belonged entirely to God. He had laid it down in death; God was raising it in life. Immediately his music took on a different quality, endowed with an unusual power. His next album soared straight to the top of the Contemporary Christian Music charts, something his music had never done. And his music influenced countless many, including me, to give away their lives for God's mission in the world.

God only raises to life what you first offer up in death.

So what is that "most precious thing" for you? A talent? A dream? Your career? Your plans for retirement?

You have to lay it down before it will be blessed with power.

A few years ago, I realized that for me, it had become my church.

Thy Kingdom Come, or My Kingdom Come?

I entered the ministry with the same ambitions many young pastors do. I sincerely wanted to reach people for Jesus, but I was also pretty interested in making a big name for myself. I wanted a large church, and I was pretty sure God was into that, too, because it seemed like a win-win for both of us.

But as we've seen, God won't bless what you claim as your own, even when it's a good thing. And so, one Friday afternoon, during a time I had set aside for prayer, God asked me if the church was mine or his. I was praying for massive revival in our city—the kind that would lead to thousands of people getting saved and would rewrite the story of our entire city. The kind they would write about one day in history books. It seemed like a good request, but as I was praying, the Spirit of God impressed something on my heart that left me speechless: "And what if I answer this prayer, sending a revival into Raleigh-Durham beyond all you've asked or imagined, one that will reshape the city for centuries—but I choose *a different* church in this city to accomplish that? What if *that* church grows, and that pastor gets famous, and your church stays the same, and you do not? And what if one day when they write the history of the movement, they never even mention you or your church?"

I knew the *right* answer to that question. I was supposed to say, "Oh, yes, Lord! You must increase, and I must decrease!" But while that may have been the right answer, it would not have been the *real* answer. I didn't just want the kingdom of God to grow, I wanted the kingdom of J. D. to grow, too. I realized that somewhere along the way, "thy kingdom come" had gotten jumbled up with "my kingdom come."

God showed me that my ministry was something that still belonged to me, and I needed to lay it down in death. By his grace, I did. And while I can't say that I've completely gotten over all sinful desires for success and acclaim, that afternoon marked a turning point in which the eyes of my heart shifted from building my kingdom to being used by God to build his.

Practically speaking, for me that has meant leading our church to give away a substantial part of our resources—both our money and leaders—for the mission of God. Around our church we regularly say, "We send our best!"

It's hard. Because, in case you don't know, the kinds of people who respond to calls to go out on church planting teams are not usually "sideline" people. They are heavily involved, giving generously, and usually leading ministries. Sending out the best of your leaders is usually in direct conflict with growing your budget and attendance.

A few years ago, I sat around a table with four of our church planting "residents," listening to the lists of those they'd recruited from our church to go on their plants. (Every year we bring onto our staff a handful of potential church planters, pay their salary for nine months, and give them one primary assignment—to recruit as many people as they can from our church to go with them.) As these four guys shared their lists of commitments with me, I heard the names of friends. Elders. Worship leaders. Key volunteers. Big givers. (Not that I know who gives what, but . . . er . . . big givers.)

I had a sick feeling in my stomach. *What are we doing? Have we thought this through? How on earth can we survive without these people?*

It was then the Spirit of God gently nudged me again, "*Whose church is this?*" This time I knew the answer. I reached my hands under the table and stretched them open before God. Quietly I prayed, "God, this is *your* church, not mine. If you want to grow us large to reach this city, so be it. But if you want to take out the best of our people and our resources to start churches elsewhere, that's okay, too. It's your church. Do with it what you will."

Just a few weeks ago we commissioned our 1,200th member to leave our church on one of our church planting teams. *Every single one* of them has been a painful loss. Trying to build community in our church sometimes feels like trying to hug a parade! But to date, those members have planted more than three hundred churches around the world. And our studies show that for every one we've sent out, there are thirty new people attending a church. I may have to wait until eternity to reunite with some of these friends we've sent out, but I'm sure when that day comes, I'll say it was worth it.

You see, what's best for the kingdom of God is not always best for us personally (in the short run!). Sometimes, you have to choose which of those you are going to prioritize.

But in order for there to be life in the world, there has to be death in you. In order for the seed of the gospel to multiply in the world, it has to be sown. Only what you give away will you keep.

The question for you is: *What precious seed has God placed in your hands?* Have you put it into God's?

As Dietrich Bonhoeffer famously said, Christ's call on our lives is not to "come and shine" or even "come and grow" but "come and die." That's how the harvest works.

The first and best of what you are has to be laid in surrender at Jesus' feet. Only then will it bring life to the world.

If we haven't done that, can we really say we are following Jesus?

There's More Than One Way to Be Wicked

The measure of discipleship is not our frequency in church or even how closely we obey the Ten Commandments. According to Jesus, the best measure of discipleship is whether we gave away our lives like seeds for the kingdom.

To not do so, Jesus said, is *wicked.* Even if you get everything else in the Christian life right.

That was the main point of one of Jesus' most famous parables, the "parable of the talents." A rich boss left behind various sums of money for his servants to invest. To one he gave five "talents"; to another, two; to another, one.

A talent was a huge sum of money—about twenty years' salary for the average day laborer.[4] So you could translate that to $10 million, $5 million, and $1 million. Then,

> "He who had received the five talents went
> at once and traded with them, and he made
> five talents more. So also he who had the two
> talents made two talents more. But he who had
> received the one talent went and dug in the
> ground and hid his master's money." (Matt.
> 25:16–18 ESV)

The guy with $10 million turned it into $20 million. The guy with $5 million into $10 million. Not too shabby. Unsurprisingly, when the boss returned, he commended them for their wise investment of his resources.

But to the one that sat on his $1 million, Jesus responded much differently:

> "You wicked and slothful servant! You knew that I reap where I have not sown and gather where I scattered no seed? Then you ought to have invested my money with the bankers, and at my coming I should have received what was my own with interest. So take the talent from him and give it to him who has the ten talents. For to everyone who has will more be given, and he will have an abundance. But from the one who has not, even what he has will be taken away. And cast the worthless servant into the outer darkness. In that place there will be weeping and gnashing of teeth." (Matt. 25:26–30 esv)

"Wicked?"

Unfruitful, ineffective, unfaithful—all these I get. But *wicked*?

What *wicked* thing had he done? He hadn't stolen the master's money or blown it on prostitutes, wild parties, gambling, or lavish living. In fact, he returned *every penny* he'd been given back to his boss.

And yet, Jesus calls this servant "wicked." Evidently, wicked is about more than what we do; it's about what we fail to do as well.

Most of us tend to think about wickedness only in terms of egregious sins. And we can certainly be wicked that way. But, according to Jesus, failing to risk our lives to their fullest potential for his kingdom is just as wicked in God's eyes as the most egregious violations of his laws.

Let that sink in for a minute.

Is it possible that Jesus regards many of us who sit faithfully in church services each weekend, keeping all of his "rules," but failing to give away our lives for his kingdom, as *wicked*?

Why Did You Fear?

Jesus shows us that ultimately the servant's failure to invest in the kingdom stemmed from a deep disregard for his Master. When called to account, he said, "Master, I know you. You're a harsh man, reaping where you haven't sown and gathering where you haven't scattered seed. So I was afraid and went off and hid your talent in the ground" (Matt. 25:24–25). His failure to risk betrayed his mistrust.

Do you want to know what keeps most people from abandoning their lives into God's kingdom, from sowing their seed into his fields?

Not stinginess, but fear.

Like this servant, they don't understand how faithful God is with what we put in his hands. His rains always come.

Which brings us back to John 12.

When Jesus spoke of the grain of seed that goes into the ground to die, he wasn't just offering a prescription for *our* ministries but a *description* of his own. Jesus would be the first one "sown in death," suffering the punishment for our sins in our place. And God faithfully responded with the rain of resurrection.

You can be sure that just as the Father was faithful to Jesus, so he will be faithful to you.

We will never be able to muster up enough strength, on our own, to risk it all for the kingdom. But the more we meditate on what happened at the cross, the more confident we will be in the God of the harvest. The cross and resurrection show us his faithfulness to send the rain of his power in response to the seed of our faith.

At the end of Paul's great chapter on the resurrection, 1 Corinthians 15, he says:

> Therefore, my dear brothers and sisters, be
> steadfast, immovable, always excelling in the
> Lord's work, because you know that your labor
> in the Lord is not in vain. (v. 58)

Death is the prerequisite for resurrection; resurrection is the promise God gives for obedience in death.

Lay down your life in surrender, and you will pick it up in power.

Give up what you cannot keep, and you'll gain what you cannot lose.

But to do so will force you to reckon with one very critical question.

≡ Chapter 6

One Thing You Lack

> "All he needed was nothing. It was the
> only thing he didn't have."
> —Sally Lloyd-Jones

My youth pastor growing up encouraged us to offer our lives as "blank checks" to God. When you give someone a blank check, you sign your name at the bottom, pre-approving whatever amount they write in later. You do this if someone doesn't know how much they need from you, so when they figure it out, they can fill in the amount and cash it.

This is always an unnerving experience for me, even when I know the person well. *What if my brother-in-law decides to empty my account and flee the country? How well do I know him, anyway?*

Essentially, this is what Jesus asks from us—that we give our lives like a blank check to him. We put our "yes" on the table, so to speak, before he even asks the question.

Most of us, however, prefer the "gift card" approach to God. With a gift card, you know exactly what you are on the hook for. When it's used up, that's not your problem. If your friend uses that $25 birthday gift card to purchase an 84-inch-high-definition TV and she still owes $1,975 on it, that's on her, not you. Gift cards allow you to remain in control of your generosity.

God won't accept gift cards. He only takes blank checks.

Alas, in recent years, when I share this illustration, more and more people look back at me with a quizzical look. *"What's a check?"* One college student told me, "I think we studied these things in my history class—'checks' . . . and phones with cords that attached to a wall and horse-drawn carriages and such—but I've never actually seen one."

So let me update the illustration: I have an app on my phone called "Venmo," which conveniently allows me to transfer money from my account to someone else's. I get to choose exactly what leaves my account. I'm in control. That's different than giving someone my bank user name and password. At that point, they are in control.

God doesn't request a Venmo relationship with us. He requires full, unrestricted access.

The only terms Jesus will accept are absolute surrender. He doesn't want our "gift cards"—whether church attendance, moral purity, generous tithes, or missionary activity. Those are all great, but more fundamentally, he wants *us*. Christian conversion is surrender, not spiritual improvement. It's like C. S. Lewis famously said, "[F]allen man is not simply an imperfect creature who needs improvement: he is a rebel who must lay down his arms."[1]

There is no "halfway" or partial surrender. Suppose a man tells his wife, that throughout their twenty years of marriage, he's been 95 percent faithful to her. That's an "A" in every school in America! Is she likely to hop up and down in glee, grateful for her "A-level" husband?

No. Ninety-five percent faithful means wholly unfaithful. Marriage is one of those relationships where partial commitment doesn't count. Neither does it in lordship. As the old saying goes, "He's either Lord *of* all, or not Lord *at* all."

Religion is the great substitute for surrender. Moral purity can sometimes mask a heart that refuses to yield control. In her novel *Wise Blood,* Flannery O'Connor describes one of her religious characters by saying, "There was already a deep black wordless conviction in him that the way to avoid Jesus was to avoid sin."[2] In other words, living in a way where you feel like you are doing a halfway decent job of keeping the rules can keep you from seeing just how desperately you need Jesus and how your only recourse is to surrender unconditionally to him.

Many people use religious activity to keep them from absolute surrender. They may be model students, spouses, and church members, but they have failed to do the "one thing" Jesus has asked of them.

The Rich Young Man

A young man came to Jesus desiring to know him, to benefit from his miraculous power, and, most of all, inherit from him eternal life. Bowing down before him, he said,

> "Good teacher, what must I do to inherit eternal life?"
>
> "Why do you call me good?" Jesus asked him. "No one is good except God alone. You know the commandments: 'Do not murder; do not commit adultery; do not steal; do not bear false witness; do not defraud; honor your father and mother.'"
>
> [The man] said to him, "Teacher, I have kept all these from my youth." (Mark 10:17–20)

You've got to hand it to this guy. It takes some serious *chutzpah* to say to the Son of God, "I've kept all the commandments, perfectly, for my whole life." Of course, Jesus knew that this wasn't true. Even if this guy kept his external life squeaky clean, he had a depraved heart, like all of us, that needed to be cleansed and transformed.

Rather than confronting his lack of self-awareness regarding his heart directly, though, Jesus decided to uncover it another way:

> Looking at him, Jesus loved him and said to him, "You lack one thing . . ." (Mark 10:21)

Now, Jesus' statement started out hopeful enough. "You lack one thing." One! Whew, what a relief! One seems completely manageable, especially for a guy who has kept all of the Ten Commandments from the time he was a boy. So what was this *one thing*?

> "Go, sell all you have and give to the poor, and
> you will have treasure in heaven. Then come,
> follow me." (Mark 10:21)

To get Jesus, this young ruler had to give up control of his money. You see, the "one thing he lacks" is not a perfect heart, but Jesus. But to get Jesus, he has to open his hands on everything else. That's the only trade God will make. John Piper explains,

> It is as though the man stood there with his
> hands full of money and Jesus said, "You lack
> one thing; reach out and take my hands." To
> do this the man must open his fingers and let
> the money fall. The "one thing" is not what
> falls out of his hands, but what he takes into his
> hands.[3]

The more you feel like you have it all together—the "richer" you are, so to speak—the less inclined you'll be to release control. Abdicating the throne of your heart usually begins with utter despair over how little you have and how much you lack.

And so, the rich young man "was dismayed by this demand, and he went away grieving, because he had many possessions" (Mark 10:22).

As Sally Lloyd-Jones wrote in *The Jesus Storybook Bible,* to get Jesus, all you need is nothing. But "nothing" is the one thing this man didn't have. So, instead of walking away with Jesus, he chose to keep clinging to his perishing riches.

I've often wondered what happened to this man later in life. When we meet him in the Gospel of Mark, he's described as a "rich young ruler." We aren't given any more of his story, but at some point he became a rich old ruler—perhaps even wealthier than when he met Jesus, but with one sorrowful statement still echoing in his mind. "One thing you lack . . ." And if he died without Jesus, he died with nothing.

Did the rich ruler live long enough to regret his decision? I hope so.

More importantly, will you?

What is that "one thing" for you?

Will you take your hands off of it so that you can take hold of him?

Do you believe that, "everything minus Jesus equals nothing"? And that, "Jesus plus nothing equals everything"?

Because believing in the core of your being is what it takes to follow him all the way.

Not the Picture I Was Looking For

I'll never forget the first time I saw a living sacrifice. In Romans 12:1, the apostle Paul said that those of us who follow Jesus should offer ourselves to him as "living sacrifices," and that always sounded poetic to me, until the first time I actually saw one. It remains one of the most disturbing experiences I've ever had.

I was living in Southeast Asia in the middle of a Muslim unreached people group. We were just concluding the fast of Ramadan, a month-long time of fasting from sun-up until sun-down. The city elders had prepared a celebratory feast marking the end of the month. I was invited to observe the rituals as a guest of honor. I was instructed to wear a clean, white shirt. I sat in the first row of a large crowd, mere feet from a large wooden altar.

Seven men brought forward the bull. Six held the hapless animal down, while one man unsheathed a long blade, holding it high for everyone to see. Then he brought the knife close to the bull's throat. And in one violent movement, he created a gaping, blood-gushing wound. Blood drenched the men attempting to hold the bull down. It sprayed all over my clothes. It began to pool on the ground, creating a disgusting slurry of mud.

Worst of all, as the blood poured out of the bull's neck, his life writhed and wheezed out along with it. Blood gushed more violently with each thrashing movement—until, suddenly, it just stopped.

The only thing more horrifying than the prolonged cacophony of agony was the sudden silence of death.

In that moment, two thoughts flooded my mind.

First, this is the image that Paul chose to describe the Christian life. I preferred triumphant images of the Christian life.

More than a conqueror.

I can do all things through Christ who strengthens me.

I like to think of the Christian life as a race where one day I'll cross the finish line, victorious and strong, with both hands raised in the air. But the image before me was not that. It was one of weakness. Waste. Gore. A picture not of a victor, but the vanquished.

Was I ready for *that* to be the picture of my life?

While this first thought unnerved me, the second one wrecked me: *This is what God, in Christ, did for me.*

Sacrifices in the Old Testament prefigured what Christ would one day do for his people. On a Friday morning nearly 2,000 years ago, Jesus went through an experience much like this poor bull, only 10,000 times worse. He was brought forward in chains, stripped naked, violently whipped in front of the crowd until his back was in tatters, then held down and fastened to a piece of wood with two rusty nails. And yet he did it all, willfully and joyfully, to absorb the curse for my sin.

Now he calls me to follow him, doing for others what he did for me.

Real Christian discipleship is hard. Surrender is hard.

But when you open your hands in surrender, you get Jesus. And he is worth it. Though you lose control of your life, you gain him.

If in your heart Christianity primarily consists of a set of rules to obey, you'll never make it. Like the rich young ruler, you may be able to keep some of the commandments for a while, but you will always lack one thing, the one thing you truly need.

Jesus.

No Substitute for Surrender

Is this a trade you are willing to make? The Christian life is not a negotiation in which God grants you eternal life and spiritual blessings in response to religious improvements you make. To get to heaven, you need Christ's righteousness, and Jesus only gives that to those willing to surrender themselves to him.

That's the only deal he's willing to make: his perfect righteousness for your total surrender.

Right after giving us the "blank check" example, my youth pastor would often say: In every heart there is a throne and a cross. If you are on the throne, Christ must be on the cross. If Christ will be on the throne, you must be on the cross.

Who is on the throne in your life? There can only be one.

Jesus doesn't come as advisor, support staff, or high counselor. He comes as reigning King or not at all.

When I was in high school, a popular bumper sticker was, "God is my copilot." It had an airplane flying across the text and the "t" in "pilot" was made to look like a cross.

Seemed spiritual. And I'm sure it brought comfort to fellow drivers. Sadly, it's a completely false picture of the Christians life.

You see, if God is your copilot, you're both in the wrong seat.

God does not come into your life as a helpful passenger to offer traveling tips, guide you out of traffic jams, and provide assistance if you get a flat tire. Nor is he your in-vehicle navigation system from whom you gain helpful route suggestions, whom you can overrule at will while he "recalculates" a new route.

When Jesus comes into your life, he pulls you over and says, "This is my car and you stole it." You get out of the driver's seat, hand him the keys, crawl in the back, and say, "You're right. The car is yours now. Where are we going?"

Many would-be-followers of Jesus, like this rich young ruler, think that the "gift cards" of improved living, mission trips, and church attendance will satisfy Jesus—like letting that person in your passenger seat pick the music. But no amount of these things will gain anyone eternal life. Just as the rich young ruler walked away from Jesus, so these Christians walk away from the life God has for them, and they might end up missing a relationship with Jesus altogether.

There is no substitute for complete and total surrender. Your only hope of salvation is the gift-righteousness of Christ, purchased for you by Jesus through his death on the cross for your sins. And he only gives that in response to total surrender.

To get him, you must give up all of you. Do you think he's worth it?

Chapter 7

Audience of One

"We ask not for riches, but look to the cross . . . .
And for our inheritance, give us the lost!"
—Bob Hartman, Petra

My favorite pre-pastor job was middle-school soccer coach. I enjoyed soccer in high school and college, so I volunteered to lead a local boys' team.

One thing I've never been accused of is approaching assignments half-heartedly, and leading this team was no exception. I believed it was my God-given mission to shape these prepubescent boys into tomorrow's leaders.

I'm not sure if I accomplished that or not, but I do know that our team was good. We blasted through the regular season without a single loss, our confidence growing with each victory. I fed this confidence every chance I got: our pre-game ritual comprised of rubbing mud on our clothes and faces, screaming battle cries, and quoting every appropriate line from *Braveheart* I could remember.

As we approached the county playoffs, my boys felt invincible. We easily dispatched the first two teams, but in the semi-finals we encountered an unexpected hurdle. The other team had a star player who was unlike any we had seen all season, far better than any of our players. It seemed that she could do whatever she wanted with a soccer ball.

That's right. I said *she*.

My little chauvinists were having a hard time accepting her athletic superiority. By the time she had scored her second goal, the mood among my guys was a combination of dismay, frustration, and confusion. She seemed untouchable. We're talking a future Mia Hamm. Serena Williams with a soccer ball.

With eleven minutes left to go in the second half, I called over our stopper, David, for a quick consultation.

"David," I said, "I am sick and tired of that girl getting open shots on our goal."

David answered, "Yes sir, coach. Me too. I hate that girl."

"Well, David, let's not go there yet," I said. "But for the remaining ten minutes you have one assignment. Only one. *She* is your assignment. Do you understand?"

David nodded.

"I don't care if the player next to you bursts into flames, David. That's not your responsibility. But if she steps foot into the penalty box with that ball, you *will not let her* get a shot off. You got it?"

Thumbs up.

As he trotted back onto the field, I called out to him, "And David, do it *legally.*" He paused, looked back quizzically, nodded, and kept running.

It was only a few minutes later when the moment of truth came. Here she came on another of her blistering runs through our defense. She flew past the midfielder like he was invisible. She juked our right fullback, leaving him cowering in the fetal position. Then she pump-faked, and our goalie jumped left, leaving the net completely open. An easy goal.

But then.

From the periphery of my vision, a small, David-shaped blur came into view. He was approaching her from her blind spot, locked onto her like a tractor beam. Just as she planted her foot to tap the ball into the goal, David tackled her, from behind. Not a legal, soccer-style "slide tackle." No, a literal, football-style, bear-hug tackle.

For a moment, it seemed that time stood still.

And then, pandemonium. Everyone, it seemed, erupted in anger. The *other* team was angry because they thought we were trying to take out their star player. Our team was angry because we'd just handed them a penalty kick in the penalty box. The ref just looked confused. *I* was screaming, since this wasn't what I had envisioned *at all.*

Our team's parents were angry because they assumed "psychocoach" had sent David in to take this girl out.

Meanwhile, with this maelstrom still swirling about him, David reached down, like a perfect little gentleman, to help this girl up. Then he turned around and looked across the field toward me, grinning like a 'possum, and gave me a huge thumbs-up.

Suddenly all of the shouting was directed at me. And one word flashed into my brain: lawsuit.

I immediately sent in a sub for David. As David came off the field, I said (looking back over my shoulder to make sure the parents could hear), "David, what was that? Where is your brain? Point to your brain. *David, what were you thinking?*"

"But, coach," David protested with a determined look of juvenile indignation, "*YOU* told me take her out *illegally*."

The last clarification David thought I had given to him as he ran out onto the field was, "David, be sure to do it *illegally*. Make it nasty."

Thankfully, the girl was fine, and I finished the season without going to jail. She scored the penalty kick and we lost 3–1. But reflecting back on that moment, I've often felt like David demonstrated, in a middle-school way, that kind of commitment Jesus calls for from all of his followers. Hear me out.

David knew this stunt would end in a penalty kick. He probably suspected he'd get yelled at by the ref and that his parents might ground him. But he went right ahead and did it anyway. That's because in his not-quite-yet-formed-preteen mind, he thought: *If coach is happy with me, everything else is gonna be okay.*

The resolve to go the distance with Jesus is sustained by the conviction that if Jesus is happy with you, you can deal with any other loss or anyone else's displeasure. His approval outshines their disapproval. His blessings outweigh their curses. His presence makes up for their loss.

Jesus said as much:

> "If anyone wants to follow after me, let him
> deny himself, and take up his cross daily, and
> follow me." (Luke 9:23)

As we saw in the last chapter, the "me" we encounter in obedience matters more than the world we leave behind.

If you're going to embrace a life of total obedience that goes the distance, you'll need to have your own "David" moment, risking it all because your divine Coach says, "Go."

You'll need, like David, to begin living for an audience of One. But unlike David, it should be One who always steers you straight and is never unclear in his instructions.

Fear Not, Little Flock

Jesus understood (and even sympathized with) the fact that living for an audience of One requires a surrender that feels terrifying. I think that's why he told his followers,

> "Don't be afraid, little flock, because your
> Father delights to give you the kingdom."
> (Luke 12:32)

I was always taught that you shouldn't mix metaphors, but here Jesus wonderfully mixes three. They constitute the trifecta of assurance. God is the a) *watchful Shepherd,* intimately aware of where we are and what we are doing; b) the *Almighty King,* controlling everything according to his good purposes in our lives; and c) a *tender Father* who delights to see us thrive.

As John Piper notes, every word of Luke 12:32 seems specifically chosen to assure us in a time of fear or uncertainty:

> [S]imply and staggeringly and unspeakably . . .
> the omnipotent rule and authority of the King
> of the universe will be engaged forever and ever
> on behalf of the little flock of God.[1]

To those wavering in their ability to obey, Jesus gave this promise because this promise is the only thing we need to walk confidently into the future. This presence is the bread upon which our souls feast in times of famine.

With these promises, what else do you need? Without them, what else would you have? Think about it:

- *Jesus is better than money.* His stock never crashes and his supply never runs low. His shelves are always full and his angels never get sick.
- *Jesus is more fulfilling than romantic love.* His are the arms you were created for.
- *Jesus is better than earthly power.* What greater power can there be than to have the sovereign God commanding every molecule in the universe for his good purposes?

- *Jesus is better than perfect health.* He offers life that sickness can't touch, pandemics can't threaten, and death can't take away.
- *Jesus is better than great accomplishments.* Hearing "well done good and faithful servant" from Jesus will count for more than 10,000 trophies that fade from memory almost the moment they are given.

We saw in the last chapter that Everything – Jesus = Nothing. Now we see that the opposite is also true.

Jesus + Nothing = Everything.

In Christ, we have the absolute assurance of the absolute approval of the only One whose opinion really matters anyway. The only promises that persevere through the passage of time. The only presence that never fails and never forsakes.

Put First Things First and He'll Throw in Second Things

Jesus knows that throughout our lives we need things like food, shelter, friends, and family. He promised to provide for our needs in abundance, but only when we put him first.

In the most famous sermon Jesus ever preached, the Sermon on the Mount, he made this promise:

> "But seek first the kingdom of God and his righteousness, and all these things will be provided for you." (Matt. 6:33)

If you read the verses that precede this one, you'll see that "all these things" means the happiness and security we crave in life.

Jesus presses this home with two analogies that correspond to two different personality types that fear the loss of different things in life. Some fear that surrendering to Jesus means they'll never be happy. To them, Jesus says,

> "Observe how the wildflowers of the field grow:
> They don't labor or spin thread. Yet I tell you
> that not even Solomon in all his splendor was
> adorned like one of these. If that's how God
> clothes the grass of the field, which is here
> today and thrown into the furnace tomorrow,
> won't he do much more for you—you of little
> faith?" (Matt. 6:28–30)

The grass of the field is the epitome of temporary. And yet God sprinkles into it gorgeous wildflowers! You, by contrast, are eternal. So, if God does this for the temporary grass, won't he also take care of you? After all, for you he gave the blood of his only Son! Can't you then trust he'll satisfy your yearnings for meaning?

A second personality type tends to fear that surrendering to God will leave them desolate. Unable to take care of themselves or their families in the future. To them, Jesus says,

> "Consider the birds of the sky: They don't sow
> or reap or gather into barns, yet your heavenly

Father feeds them. Aren't you worth more than
they?" (Matt. 6:26)

Birds don't save for the future. They don't huddle around
Fox News or CNN every night anxiously worried about where
society is headed. And yet, God pours out all kinds of abundance
on them, too. Surely you and I—sons and daughters of God,
made in his image, redeemed by the blood of his Son—are worth
more to God than the birds. So, if that's how God takes care of
his birds, can't you rest secure that he'll take great care of his
children, too?

Chances are, you'll find yourself in one of these two personality types. When you think about total and unconditional
surrender of your life to God, what fear rises most quickly in
your heart? Is it that you'll never be as happy as you could be if
you were in charge, or that somehow you'll end up abandoned,
desolate, and needy?

Generally speaking, when it comes to money, people fall into
one of these two personality types. There are those for whom
money is happiness. So when they get a little extra, they *spend* it.
There are others for whom money is security. So when they get a
little extra, they *save* it. In God's sense of humor, these two kinds
of people always get married to each other, and both think that
the other one has a problem with money. When they get an extra
thousand dollars, the spender wants a new TV, and the saver
wants to start a mutual fund. That's because for the spender,
money is the way to satisfaction in the present; for the saver, it's
the way to security for the future.

To both groups, Jesus says, "Put me—instead of your happiness and security—first, and I'll supply more of both of those things than you could ever hope for."

Matthew 6:33 is the closest thing I have to a life verse. My dad gave it to me before I left for college. "Son," he said, "*all these things* includes the money to live. It includes satisfaction in your career. It includes a marriage partner (if that's what God has for you) and fulfilling friendships. Those are all wonderful things, but seek all of them *second*. Seek God first and he'll add those things to you."

I love how C. S. Lewis summarized it: He said in life there are first things (God and his will) and second things (everything else we think we need for a successful, happy life). If we put first things first, Lewis says, Jesus promises to throw in second things. But put second things first, and we'll lose not only the first things but eventually the second things too.[2] The money you gave your life to leaves you feeling empty and insecure. The marriage doesn't last. The friends are no longer around.

By contrast, if surrendering to God means that marriage is not what he has for you, or following him includes the loss of a good job or abandonment by some of your friends, Jesus promises to make up those losses in other ways. He said,

> "Truly I tell you, there is no one who has left a
> house, wife or brothers or sisters, parents or chil-
> dren because of the kingdom of God, who will
> not receive many times more at this time, and
> eternal life in the age to come." (Luke 18:29–30)

It is the universal testimony of Christians in every age that when God leads you to a place where your earthly needs are wanting, he more than makes up for it. As Holocaust survivor Corrie Ten Boom put it, "Every experience God gives us, every person He puts in our lives is the perfect preparation for a future that only He can see."[3] Sometimes he supplies our needs in ways we were not expecting. Sometimes he supplies that need in himself. As King David found, when God prepares us a table in the presence of our enemies, even there our cup overflows (Ps. 23:5).

When you set your life to pursue anything else, however, it ultimately lets you down.

Rusty Isn't Real

The great irony of life without God is that you usually don't end up enjoying the things you pursued in his place. It's only by having him in the right place that you develop the right relationship with all the second-place things.

It reminds me of a story a friend of mine told me about his first trip to the local greyhound racing track.

Right before a race starts, he told me, they bring out a mechanical rabbit named Rusty who runs back and forth on a little track in front of the dogs. The crowd goes crazy and the announcer bellows, "Heeeeeeeeere's Rusty!" Those dogs get pumped! They start banging against the doors of the cages, itching to get ahold of Rusty. And when the gates open a couple of seconds later, they tear off after Rusty like their lives depend on catching him. He runs in front of them all the way to the finish line, where he suddenly disappears into a little hole in the ground. Every time.

You have to imagine that later, as they're lounging back in the kennel, one of them is like, "Ahh, but I was *so close* to getting Rusty this time!" And his friends respond, "Me too! You think we'll ever see him again?" Sure enough, the next day, Rusty's back! Every day, the same dogs chase the same rabbit that they never catch.

We think, "What dumb dogs! Don't they realize the whole thing is rigged? The rabbit is not even real!"

But for many of us, when our alarm goes off in the morning, it might as well blare out, "Heeeeeeeeere's Rusty!" Our feet hit the floor and we're off around the track.

Occasionally, my friend told me, something goes wrong with the mechanical rabbit and one of the dogs actually catches him. He chews through it and realizes (in his doggie way), "Hey, wait a minute. I've been duped. This whole thing is a fraud." If that happens, he says, that dog never races with quite the same vigor again.

And—brace yourself—that's where the dogs might actually be smarter than us. You see, many of us have caught the "Rusty" we set out after. We got the car, moved into the house, and nabbed the corner office we had set our eyes on. But as we chew through one blessing, realizing it's not all we thought it was, we think, *Oh no! I must have chosen the wrong rabbit. I'll find another one.* We choose a new girlfriend, a different career, a new goal, or a more expensive house. We chew through one blessing after another, each one leaving us emptier than the one before.

Chasing "Rusty" leads to a life of incessant running and perpetual exhaustion. Chase after God, however, and he'll surprise you with so much joy, abundance, and satisfaction that you won't know how to contain it all.

Again, C. S. Lewis said it best:

> The [things] in which we thought the beauty
> was located will betray us if we trust to them;
> it was not *in* them, it only came *through* them,
> and what came through them was longing.
> These things . . . are good images of what we
> really desire; but if they are mistaken for the
> thing itself they turn into dumb idols, break-
> ing the hearts of their worshippers. For they are
> not the thing itself; they are only the scent of a
> flower we have not found, the echo of a tune we
> have not heard, news from a country we have
> never yet visited.[4]

The happiness and security we yearn for is not in these other things. They are good gifts of God designed to point us toward the Source of satisfaction and security. But when we treat them as though they are the source of satisfaction and security, they leave us broken and empty.

Ask yourself: *How would my life change if I realized the rabbit wasn't real?*

If He Supplied the Greater, We Can Trust Him for the Lesser

Resigning your pursuit of second things and putting Jesus first is definitely a difficult leap of faith. If you're having trouble with it, take a step back and consider the One who beckons you to follow. He's a God who submitted himself to humiliation, torture, and death to rescue you from your sin. He loved you before you loved him, and loved you more completely than anyone else ever has. Don't you think you can trust him with the rest of your life?

This is the logic Paul employs in Romans 8:

> He did not even spare his own Son but gave
> him up for us all. How will he not also with
> him grant us everything? (v. 32)

Surely if he supplied the greater, we can trust him for the lesser. As David declares in the Psalms, "no good thing does he withhold" from those who trust him (Ps. 84:11 ESV). This is proven by the fact that he did not withhold grace when we deserved wrath, and offered to us the most valuable gift in the universe: his Son.

No one discards things of great value to them, and we know that we are of great value to God by the price he paid to redeem us. The value of something is shown by what someone is willing to pay for it. (Pastor Joby Martin calls it the "eBay rule." You may have something in your house that you feel is incredibly valuable. But when you put it on eBay, you find out it's worth about $6 to everybody else. That signed collection of Hannah Montana posters? It's your greatest childhood prize. But the online community is not very impressed.)

Or sometimes it works in reverse. You have something you barely even think about, but then someone is willing to pay you a huge amount for it and it shifts your whole attitude. When my grandmother died, we discovered an ordinary-looking, stained-glass lamp in her living room. We took it with a big pile of other junk to an antique store to see what we could get for the lot. The guy at the antique store offered us $25,000, just for the lamp. I'm not kidding. I wanted to take it in the back and rub it to see if a genie came out. We had no idea. My grandmother had no idea. (Though it was conspicuous how many people "suddenly remembered" that Granny had promised the lamp to them!) My first thought was of all those times my sister and I had played dodgeball in that room. None of us understood the lamp's true value until we saw what someone was willing to pay for it.

God purchased you at an unfathomable price. He gave the blood of his Son *for you*. And Paul reasons that if God did that,

> Would he really withhold from us help in our
>   marriages?
>
> Why would he withhold from us wisdom in
>   our parenting?
>
> Why would he not provide for our futures?

It's the simplest logic in the universe. If he has put into us the blood of his Son, he's not going to waste us.

So,

> *Don't be afraid, little flock, because your Father*
> *delights to give you the kingdom.*

I'm Not Afraid of This Fire

The more we stand assured of this heavenly promise, the less terrified we are of earthly loss. Losses in life, though painful, are light and momentary.

Polycarp lived in the second century AD and had the privilege of being discipled personally by the apostle John. But John was long gone when Roman authorities showed up on February 23, AD 155 at Polycarp's house in the city of Smyrna to haul him away and burn him at the stake for his repeated refusals to stop preaching the gospel of Jesus. Polycarp was eighty-six years old.

He asked for a moment to pray, which witnesses say he did very calmly. Even the soldiers, they say, were moved by his serenity. Then, motioning toward the bundle of wood and torches nearby, he declared, "Eighty-six years I have served Christ, and he never did me any wrong. How can I blaspheme my King who saved me?"

The officials tied Polycarp to the pyre. Just before they lit the wood, they asked him if he had any last words. He glanced at the gathering crowd, and then lifted his voice to a shout: "You think I am afraid of this fire? The fire you threaten lasts only an hour and is quenched. But what do you know of the fires of judgement? So come on boys, bring on the fire!"[5]

As John Wesley famously put it, "The one who fears God need fear nothing else."

If he says "well done," you have the approval of the only One whose opinion really matters. If he stands by your side, it is inconsequential who stands in front of you. If he's in your corner, the fight is over.

Jesus + Nothing = Everything.

Chapter 8

Do People Really Need to Hear about Jesus to Get to Heaven?

"The gospel is only good news if it gets there in time."
—CARL F. H. HENRY

It's rare, even today, to find an American citizen who knows virtually nothing about Jesus. But that was Rhonda.

Rhonda grew up in New England. I shared my testimony with her, and she asked me questions ranging from the sincere to the sarcastic.

So I started with the basics—who God was, why Jesus had come, and why we could only be saved through him. But then she asked me something I wasn't expecting:

"You *actually* believe this?"

"Well . . . yes," I said.

She replied, "Because you don't *act* like you believe it."

She went on: "If I believed what you *say* you believe—that everyone in my life who didn't know Jesus was separated from God's love and headed to eternity in hell—I'm not sure how I could make it through the day! I would *constantly* be on my knees, *pleading* with people to listen."

"But you," she said, "you just act like you are trying to win a debate with me. Trying to demonstrate that your way of looking at the world is superior to mine. Not that we are talking about matters of eternal life and death."

I'm not sure I've ever felt so dumbstruck. I knew she was right, and I wasn't sure how to respond. How is it possible to believe the gospel and not be *crushed* with a sense of urgency?

Ambiguity about the state of people in the world without Jesus keeps many Christians from truly leveraging their lives in ways that impact eternity. It keeps them from seeing how urgent the moment is and how important are the decisions we make about what to do with our lives.

Perhaps we know the right theological answers to such questions and simply numb ourselves to their meaning. But I also suspect that many of us are not convinced, deep in our hearts, that Jesus really is the only way to enter heaven. We ask: How could God hold people responsible for information they never even had a chance to hear?

Deep down, it just doesn't seem fair. Is God really going to appear at someone's bedside the moment they die, we muse, and declare, "Aha! You didn't believe in Jesus!" And they say, "Jesus who?" To which he replies, "It's too late now!" And as he casts their souls down into hell, they call back, "But I never heard about Jesus . . ." To which he mutters back "tough cookies" in Latin or something like that. And that just seems unfair.

So we quietly speculate that there are perhaps other ways. God probably grades on the curve. I suspect that for many Christians, while their declared creed might be orthodox, functionally they are universalists (believing that sincere people of every religion go to heaven).

The apostle Paul appears to have struggled with this question, too, as he devotes several chapters in the book of Romans to answering it. He is explaining to the Roman Christians why he is so driven to get the gospel not only to Rome but from there to the ends of the earth—even if that costs him inconvenience, imprisonment, torture, and death.

It's hard to imagine someone going through all that to get the gospel to people who would still go to heaven if they died having never heard it. So Paul explains why extreme measures to get the gospel to the ends of the earth are warranted.

I want to walk you through the logic of Paul's explanation, and show you how, in light of it, the only proper response to people without Christ is a life-captivating sense of urgency.

The Six Premises of an Eternal Worldview[1]

Premise 1: All people have heard about God and rejected him.

In reality, there is no one who is unfamiliar with God. In Romans 1, Paul writes,

> For God's wrath is revealed from heaven against all godlessness and unrighteousness of people who by their unrighteousness *suppress* the truth, since what can be known about God is evident among them, because God has shown it to them. For his invisible attributes, that is, his eternal power and divine nature, have been clearly seen since the creation of the world, being understood through what he has made. As a result, people are without excuse. (vv. 18–20, emphasis mine)

Paul's argument that all people have heard about God hinges on the word *suppress*. Suppression is not the same as ignorance. *Suppression* means that we deny something we instinctively know to be true.

The truth about God's authority, glory, and holiness, Paul says, is evident all around us, testified to us through both the splendor of creation and the instinctive convictions of our hearts.

The problem is that the posture of our hearts leans toward "godlessness" (a hateful attitude toward God) and "unrighteousness" (a selfish attitude toward our fellow humans). Therefore, we don't like the witness of creation or our consciences and don't want it to be true. The truth about God's glory conflicts with our desire for our own glory; the truth about his holiness with our sense of our own goodness; and the truth about his authority with our desire to do whatever we want.

And so, we suppress the truth our hearts instinctively know. That suppression expresses itself in one of three forms:

1. We *rebel* against the truth we acknowledge. Paul uses the Jews as an example here: Though they knew the Ten Commandments, no one truly kept them. Everyone, in ways big and small, turns aside to their own ways.

2. We *distort* the truth we perceive. We reshape God into a deity we can manage and manipulate. This, Paul explains, is the place from where false religions spring. We concoct deities and religious philosophies to accommodate our sinful and self-serving impulses.

3. We *deny* the truth altogether. We develop God-free philosophies like atheism or agnosticism. We're not always aware that this is suppression, either. Just as a bigoted person finds reasons to hate a group of people they already don't like, we find reasons to disbelieve God. Perhaps you say, "But

> I know an atheist that is *genuinely* intel-
> lectually convinced that there is no God."
> Paul would say, "Sure. But the reason their
> minds were able to convince them of that
> is because that is what their hearts wanted
> to be true." Imagine a racist who finds
> continual evidence to support his convic-
> tion that another race of people is inferior
> to his own. His perception of the evidence
> is driven by the hatred in his heart. That's
> how we are with God. Our heart sees only
> what it wants to see.

When it comes to knowledge about God, no one in the world is completely ignorant. We are all born with a sense of the divine. We experience that through feelings of moral account-ability or in our transcendent longings for meaning and immor-tality. These yearnings are universal. The very complexity and beauty of creation give us a sense of the power and majesty of the God behind it all. We may never have heard his name, but our hearts instinctively know he is there.

Helen Keller was born blind, deaf, and mute. For the first several years of her life, it was as if she existed in a dark, silent room. Annie Sullivan famously took on the responsibility to teach her to communicate. After working with her for years, she taught her to communicate through a series of signs she pressed into her hand. When Keller was a teenager, Annie Sullivan wanted to teach her about God. As she tried to describe him,

Keller became very excited and signed back, "Oh, is that what you call him? I always knew he was there, I just didn't know what his name was."[2]

The problem is, apart from God's grace at work in us, none of us truly *want* him to be there. At least, not in a way where we devote our lives to his glory and authority. As one philosopher put it: "We know, but we don't know because we don't want to know."[3] The human race, as a whole, refuses to acknowledge the truth about God because we don't like what it demands of us.

Premise 2: God has rightfully condemned all.

If, as Paul claims, we each have suppressed the knowledge of God by rebellion, distortion, and denial, then we each deserve the wrath of God. Right? If we willfully put our fist in God's face and say, "Get off the throne. I belong there," how could we expect anything less?

Paul says that though we may have never uttered those words, how we each choose to *live* says that to God. Our suppression, whether it comes in the form of rebellion, distortion, or denial, is rooted in a heart-level hatred of God's glory and authority.

All of us are guilty, you see, not because of what we *don't* know, but because of what we *did* know and rejected.

Or, to state it another way: God doesn't condemn people for not hearing about Jesus. He condemns them for suppressing, distorting, and rejecting the knowledge of God that they knew in their hearts.

God will not appear at anyone's bedside as an unrecognized stranger. Paul declares that we all knew he was there, even if we didn't know what to call him. We all will recognize him as the God whose authority we hated and resisted.

Paul concludes his analysis of the human race with these words:

> All have turned away; all alike have become
> [spiritually] worthless. There is no one who
> does what is good, [none who seeks God,] not
> even one. (Rom. 3:12)

Let the force of those last three words hit you: Not. Even. One.

So when we ask, "What about the innocent tribesman on a remote island who is pure in heart and spirit, but who just never heard about God?"

God replies: Not. Even. One.

No person born to the human race ever had a righteous, God-pleasing heart. Well, except for One. And he's the subject of our next premise.

Premise 3: In grace, God has made a way of salvation for all.

God could have left us in the darkness and death and desolation of our situation. He would have been completely justified to do that. He could have left us with hearts coiled up in a posture of resistance and hatred.

He could have, but didn't.

In Christ, God came to earth to live the life we were supposed to live (a sinless life) and die the death we had been condemned to die. He took our sin and offered us his righteousness for our salvation, available to all who will simply receive it as a gift:

> But now, apart from the law, the righteousness
> of God has been revealed, attested by the Law
> and the Prophets. The righteousness of God is
> through faith in Jesus Christ to all who believe.
> (Rom. 3:21–22)

This was an act of sheer grace, Paul says—totally *undeserved* favor (Rom. 3:24–26). Salvation is not a reward for rightly responding to God. It's an act of grace that God bestows on people who acknowledge they don't deserve it.

Premise 4: People have to hear about this gift to receive it.

This is the crux of Paul's argument. He writes,

> How, then, can they call on him they have not
> believed in? And how can they believe without
> hearing about him? (Rom. 10:14)

In order to believe in Jesus and receive salvation, someone has to hear about him. It's like Martin Luther once said, "It wouldn't matter if Jesus died 1,000 times if no one ever heard about him," or to use the words of Carl F. H. Henry: "The gospel is only good news if it gets there in time."[4]

Perhaps you say, "Well, what if someone never heard about Jesus but they responded to what they saw of God in creation or in their conscience—or maybe the good and true parts of their religion—in the right way? What if, awed by the majesty of creation, they looked up and said, *'God, or Great Spirit in the sky—whatever or whoever you are—I don't know much about you, but I want to know you and surrender to you'*—wouldn't that be enough?"[5]

The trouble is that none of us, as we've seen, apart from the grace of God responds to the knowledge of God that way.

Interestingly though, Scripture does seem to indicate that if someone ever does respond the right way to God, God will get the rest of the gospel message to them. We see that, for example, in the story of Cornelius, recorded in Acts 10:

> There was a certain man . . . called Cornelius, a centurion of what was called the Italian Regiment, a devout man and one who feared God with all his household, who gave alms generously to the people, and prayed to God always. About the ninth hour of the day he saw clearly in a vision an angel of God coming in and saying to him, "Cornelius!" And when he observed him, he was afraid, and said, "What is it, lord?" So he said to him, "Your prayers and your alms have come up for a memorial before God. Now send men to Joppa, and send for . . . Peter. (Acts 10:1–5 NKJV)

First, realize that if salvation were possible apart from hearing the gospel, certainly Cornelius would have qualified. He responded positively to the revelation he had been given. But the angel God sent to him didn't declare that he was "already saved."

Instead, he told him to send for Peter so he could hear the message about how to be saved.

Peter didn't declare to Cornelius that he was an "anonymous Christian"[6] with implicit faith who simply needed to have the details filled in. Instead, he declared to Cornelius, "All the prophets testify about him that *through his name* everyone who *believes in him* receives forgiveness of sins" (Acts 10:43, emphasis mine). Cornelius then believed, and was saved (Acts 10:44).

This passage affirms that it is necessary to hear the message of the gospel and believe it to be saved, but it also indicates that if there is someone out there whom God enables to respond in the right way to the knowledge that they have, God will raise up someone to get the rest of the message to them.

Which leads us to premise five.

Premise 5: We are the only ones from whom they can hear it.

Paul writes,

> And how can they hear without a preacher?
> And how can they preach unless they are sent?
> (Rom. 10:14–15)

The only way they can hear is from a "preacher." And "preachers" are us humans commissioned with the message.

Throughout the book of Acts, we only ever see the gospel proclaimed from human mouths. Even (as in the case of Cornelius) when it would have been easier for an angel to share it.

Think about it: Why not have the angel who appeared to Cornelius go ahead and share the rest of the message? Evidently, angels sharing the gospel is "against the rules." God spreads the good news of salvation for fallen humans only through the mouths of other men. The angel therefore sent Cornelius to Peter, who finished the job.

Here's where it gets exciting. God's Spirit is stirring in the hearts of people like Cornelius all around the world, convicting them of sin and putting in their hearts a yearning to know him. Sometimes he even sends angelic messengers to them, or dreams and visions, with instructions for how they might seek him. But they can only hear the actual gospel message from us.

Which leads me to this question: *What if the reason God is moving in you right now* **here** *is that he is moving in someone else* **there** *to whom he wants to send you?*

I ask that because I once met a "Cornelius."

Right after college, I spent two years as a missionary in Southeast Asia. One of the first guys I got to know there was "Ishmael." He befriended me, taught me the local language and customs, and was as hospitable a person as I have ever known. He volunteered as a youth worker at his local mosque.

I shared the gospel with Ishmael at least a dozen times. Each time, he would put his hand on my shoulder and say, "J. D., my brother, you are a great man of faith, and I know your zeal for God makes your parents very proud. You are a Christian because you were born a Christian. I am a Muslim because I was born a Muslim. Islam is God's path for me."

About a week before I came home, I met with him one last time to plead that he consider Jesus' exclusive claims about salvation. He responded as he had before: "Islam is the path God has for me."

The day that I was to leave, Ishmael showed up at my house unexpectedly. I could tell something was on his mind. He told me that after our last conversation, he had not been able to shake my words. He said, "They sat on my heart like a great weight."

He then told me about a vision he had later that same night. He saw in a dream a road springing up before him, stretching to heaven, and—to his surprise, he said—*I* was on it. (In fact, he seemed *so* surprised by the fact that I was on it that I was almost a little offended!) He watched me walk up to the gates of heaven. But the doors were closed.

"But then," he said with surprise, "Someone inside knew your name!" The gates opened, he said, and I went in.

"And my heart broke," he said, "because I really wanted to go with you."

"But then the doors opened a second time, and you walked back down to earth, reached out your hand to me, pulled me onto your back, and carried me back up into heaven with you."

He then looked at me and said, "At first, I thought this was a dream that came from eating 'strange fish.'" No kidding. That's actually what he said. "But I have had enough of those dreams to know that this was not that. This was a dream from God! Do you think so? What do you think my dream means?"

Side note: I was raised in a really traditional Baptist church and we didn't offer a class on "dreams and the interpretations thereof." But I am happy to report that in that moment I knew *exactly* what to say.

I explained to him that Jesus was the way, the truth, and the life.

Sadly, he still couldn't bring himself to believe. It was just too much for him, and to my knowledge, to this day he hasn't come to faith. Several members of his family died a few years later in the 2004 Southeast Asian tsunami, but he survived, and I have looked for him several times since then. I hope one day I will have the privilege of leading him to Jesus. You can pray with me about that.

But it was the thing he said next that will forever haunt me. He said, "I know that this dream means that you were sent here by God to show me the way of salvation, to help me find it. But you are going home, and you are the only Christian I have ever known."

There are Corneliuses all around the world in whom God is stirring. But they can only come to faith through the witness of one of us. Maybe that is the reason he is stirring in you right now. Maybe it's why you picked up this book. Which leads me to the last premise.

Premise 6: The task is urgent.

This is the heart of the matter: *If the gospel is true, how should we then live?*

Because here's the reality: Only a third of the people on earth even *claim* to be Christians. That means at least 4.5 billion are undeniably lost. About half of them qualify as "unreached"— which means that they have no realistic chance (as things stand now) of hearing the gospel before they die.

If you lined up these people five across, they would circle the globe five times. Get that picture in your mind: a vast throng of people, larger than any you've ever seen, marching headlong into a hopeless eternity.

Four-and-a-half *billion*. Please don't just read that number as a statistic.

Joseph Stalin once said that we hear of the death of one as a tragedy but the death of a million as just a statistic. That's a chilling statement coming from him, but he meant that when you look into the face of one who is suffering you tend to feel compassion because you see in that person someone just like you. Say "million" or "billion" and you no longer think of them that way.

Yet each one of those *billions* is some*one* just like you and me. Someone made in the image of God. Someone with hopes and dreams and fears. Someone who knows what it's like to feel alone. Someone who likely was loved by their parents. Someone for whom going to hell will be every bit the tragedy as it would be for you or for me.

Doesn't that reality demand something from us?

God loved these people enough to suffer death on their behalf. Do we love them, and him, enough to tell them about him?

We Are Debtors Indeed

The apostle Paul said that in light of this, giving his life to spread the gospel was a debt he owed to those who hadn't heard (Rom. 1:14).

Debtor is an interesting word. Paul had never even met these people. How could he feel in debt to them?

Well, there's two ways to be in someone's debt. If you've borrowed something from them, you owe them. But you can also owe them because someone gave you something to give to them.

Say you worked for "Feed the Children" and had been given a donation of $1 million. Instead of putting the money to work feeding children, you put it in your own account and lived off the interest. Someone would rightfully say, "That is *stealing.* The money wasn't given to you for you; it was given to you for *them*."

That's how Paul felt about the gospel. Paul knew he didn't deserve to hear the gospel any more than anybody else did—he was just as much of a God-rejecter as anyone else. God's selection of him for grace was an undeserved privilege. With that privilege came the responsibility to share it with others.

As I've heard my friend David Platt say, "Every saved person this side of heaven *owes* the gospel to every unsaved person this side of hell."

For many years I struggled with the "fairness" of the gospel. I thought it was unfair of God to condemn those who hadn't heard. But as Romans taught me, our condemnation is fair. What is *not* fair, however, is that those of us who know the grace of God do nothing to get to those who don't.

It's not fair for those of us who have heard so much to do so little to get the message about a God who has done everything to those who have heard nothing at all.

Charles Spurgeon was once asked by one of his students the question we've considered in this chapter, whether those who had never heard about Jesus could be saved. "A troubling question indeed," he replied. "But even more troubling was whether we who knew the gospel and were doing nothing to bring it to the lost could be saved."

Where does that leave us? I believe it demands two things of us all.

First, live sent to the people in your life. In Acts 17 Paul explained that God arranges even the borders of nations to give people in those nations a chance to hear. That means where you live, where you work, and whom you know is no accident. God arranged those things so that he could put you around people who needed to hear. They can't believe in Jesus until you've told them about him.

He's put you at a post, his emissary to a precious group of people whom he loves. Don't fail them.

Second, consider crossing a boundary. It's always easiest to stick with sharing only to your roommate, your coworker, and the people on your sports team. But in order for the gospel to get to people who have never heard, somebody has to cross boundaries. And crossing boundaries is almost always uncomfortable and unnatural.

But the only reason you and I have the gospel today is because someone crossed that uncomfortable and inconvenient cultural boundary to get it to us. The gospel didn't start in the English-speaking world. Thank God for those men and women who crossed boundaries, often at the cost of their lives, to bring the gospel from Jerusalem to the ends of the earth! Without them, where would you and I be?

The answer is, of course: *The exact same place billions still are without you.*

Would you ask God if he is calling you to cross a geographical or cultural boundary to take the gospel to people unlike you—to other parts of the city, and perhaps other parts of the world?

Lots of people still need Jesus in the Western world, of course, but if someone here in Raleigh, North Carolina, where I live wants to hear the gospel, they can go to one of the 2,000-plus churches in our city! Or they can tune into any number of gospel programs on radio, TV, or the internet. Christian books appear on the shelves of almost every bookstore, and Christian movies cycle through local theatres on a regular basis.

Yet, at the same time, two billion people will go to bed tonight in a place where they couldn't access the message even if they wanted to.

Of course you need to be *called* to go. But here's the other side of that: *You also need to be called to stay.* Wherever you are, you should be called there and feel "sent" to there. Based solely on the math, it seems to me that the burden of proof lies on us to show why we're called to stay in a place with so much when there are so many places that have so little.

This was the sentiment that produced the greatest missions movement in Western history, the Student Volunteer Movement. In one year, the movement produced more missionaries than had been sent from the United States in the preceding century. Robert Wilder, one of the movement's leaders, said that instead of saying, "We will stay unless God sends us," we should say, "We will go unless God stops us."[7]

If you are called to stay, like I am for now, be every bit as committed to the Great Commission as those who go. John Piper says that when it comes to the Great Commission, there are only three options: go, send, or disobey. And those of us called to send need to be every bit as committed as those who go.

William Carey famously told the English Baptists before he left for India at the end of the eighteenth century: *"I will dangle from the rope as your representative in India, but you have to commit to holding securely to the other end."*

You need to look at your resources, your networks, and your opportunities, through the lens of eternity and ask, "Why, God, did you give me these?" And then leverage them for maximum gospel impact.

We only get one shot at this life, one shot to make the most of our mist. Don't waste it.

Is Your "Yes" on the Table?

Every New Year my wife and I take a week to ask God if this is the year he wants us to leave our home in the United States to take the gospel somewhere around the world. So far, each year, God has said "no." Or "not yet."

Maybe next year he'll answer "Yes." We're ready. Our "yes" is on the table; we are ready for God to put it on the map—be that in Raleigh, North Carolina, or in Bandung, Indonesia, or somewhere in between.

Will you join us in that prayer? It could be the gateway to an impact you'll never regret.

What are you doing with your life?

Chapter 9

Worth It

> "It is not the critic who counts. . . . The credit belongs
> to the man who is actually in the arena, whose face
> is marred by dust and sweat and blood; who strives
> valiantly; who errs, who comes short again and again . . .
> who spends himself for a worthy cause; who, at the best,
> knows in the end the triumph of high achievement, and
> who, at the worst, if he fails, at least fails while daring
> greatly, so that his place shall never be with those cold
> and timid souls who neither know victory nor defeat."
> —THEODORE ROOSEVELT

Have you ever seen "cardboard testimonies"? Basically, to the backdrop of a worship song, people walk across a stage holding a piece of cardboard. On one side is a one-sentence description of their life before Christ. Something like:

"Broken and alone."

"In bondage to the opinions of others."

"Self-hater."

After a moment, they flip their cardboard over, revealing a one-sentence description of their life after Christ:

"Rescued and recommissioned."

"Set free."

"Beloved daughter."

The best one I've ever seen was a woman whose front side read, "Diagnosed with stage-4 breast cancer." She was joined by an older man on stage who held up his sign, "Doctor who diagnosed her. Atheist."

Then he flipped over his sign, which read,

"Through her joy in suffering, came to know Christ."

Then, she flipped over hers:

"Worth it."

Worth it.

I really want to be able to say those words at the end of my life.

We admire—even envy—the athlete who suffers through seemingly endless hours of training to master his game. I always loved that moment in the Rocky Balboa movies where Rocky endured whatever brutal training his coach laid out for him so he could face whatever mammoth of a man awaited him in the ring. It was inspiring to watch him try to run through two feet of snow, do sit-ups off the loft of a barn and chase chickens, because you knew the moment would come where he would step into the ring chiseled up like a Greek god. When they played the Rocky theme song and he dropped his robe, you knew that every moment of agonizing training was worth it.

We admire the discipline of the student who labors into the wee hours of the night to get the degree. Or the Navy Seal who endures the incomprehensible torments of "hell week" to become one of our country's elite warriors. We praise the devotion of the single mother who tirelessly works two jobs to get her kids through school.

We know that, painful as their journeys may be, there will come a time when each of these crosses the finish line, collapses in triumph, and says, "Worth it."

Imagine being able to live with a sense of purpose so compelling that even your darkest days of struggle brim with that hope, confident that the day will come when you look back over every difficult circumstance, every dark chapter, and say *worth it*.

"I Can Trust My Good Father Even with a Blindfold in His Hands"

There's a young mother in my church, whom I'll call Kristen, who last year went in for a routine eye exam when she received devastating news.

The doctor told her that she had developed a degenerative and incurable condition that would take her sight in less than five years. She had no idea anything was even wrong! Kristen is in her mid-thirties, and she has four children, two biological and two adopted. If things go as the doctors predict, she'll never see them graduate.

Just a couple of weeks before the doctor visit, Kristen had asked God to guide her to a "theme verse" for the year. God had led her to 2 Corinthians 4:16–18:

> Therefore we do not give up. Even though our outer person is being destroyed, our inner person is being renewed day by day. For our momentary light affliction is producing for us an absolutely incomparable eternal weight of glory. So we do not focus on what is seen, but on what is unseen. For what is seen is temporary, but what is unseen is eternal.

Kristen had written in her journal, *"God, help me to trust in things not seen. Help me to fix my eyes, thoughts, and affections not on the temporary, but on the eternal. I want a faith that depends on you at every turn and eyes that are focused on you."*

Here's what she shared with me:

> As I listened to the news of my diagnosis, I heard in my heart God speak over me truth: "So we do not focus on what is seen, but on what is unseen. For what is seen is temporary,

but what is unseen is eternal." This is not an affliction God has done to me, but something he has entrusted to my stewardship. I was reminded of Jesus' words to his disciples when *they* came across a blind man: This has come to pass so that the work of God could be displayed.

God has shown me more of him in the midst of this suffering. Looking back on that prayer from January 2019, I realize now that God was preparing me to hear this news. Already God has used this diagnosis to help me fix my eyes on him, to help me to depend on him, to grow my spiritual sight. Jesus is far sweeter and more valuable in suffering than when I think I can do life on my own. And as painful as it has been, I'm learning what it means that my spiritual sight is far more valuable than my physical sight.

I do not bank my hope on any healing for my coming blindness, as there is none. I bank my hope on the suffering Savior, Jesus Christ, who is far more precious than sight, or my ability to drive, or walk independently, or see my four children's faces. These things are inconsequential in light of eternity.

Shortly after my diagnosis, I was praying when I saw a vision in my mind. Jesus was leading me, blindfolded, in the midst of the most beautiful landscape I've ever seen. Once I got to an overlook, Jesus took my blindfold off. In that moment, I realized God was showing me I can trust my good Father, even with a blindfold in his hands. I can give up my sight for a short time here on earth because I trust my Father knows what's best for me, always working for my good and for his glory. Because what is seen is temporary and what is unseen is eternal.

Worth it.

Heaven's Standing Ovation

"Worth it" is the conviction that inflamed the first Christian martyr, Stephen.

Stephen had been hauled into court to give an account of his actions. Because of his sacrificial service to poor widows, many Jewish priests were turning to faith in Christ. There before the angry Sanhedrin, he explained that everything he did, he did as an act of worship to Christ. And then,

When they [the religious leaders] heard these things, they were enraged and gnashed their teeth at him. Stephen, full of the Holy Spirit, gazed into heaven. He saw the glory of God, and Jesus standing at the right hand of God. He

said, "Look, I see the heavens opened and the
Son of Man standing at the right hand of God!"

They yelled at the top of their voices, cov-
ered their ears, and together rushed against him.
They dragged him out of the city and began to
stone him. And the witnesses laid their gar-
ments at the feet of a young man named Saul.
While they were stoning Stephen, he called out,
"Lord Jesus, receive my spirit!" He knelt down
and cried out with a loud voice, "Lord, do not
hold this sin against them!" And after saying
this, he [died]. (Acts 7:54–60)

What's most peculiar about Stephen's vision is that he sees
Jesus *standing*. Everywhere else you see Jesus at the right hand of
God he is *sitting*. It's actually an important theological symbol—
Jesus' being seated indicates that the work of salvation is done. So
why would Jesus here be standing?

I think there's only one possible explanation: he's standing to
honor his son and receive him home.

The world has just labeled Stephen a traitor, and they are
throwing baseball-sized stones at him to prove it. Jesus—it's
almost like he can't help it—stands to his feet and says, "No!
He's my son." They jeered, "Your life is a waste." Jesus responded,
"Well done, good and faithful servant."

And Stephen, face beaming with angelic brightness, felt one
overpowering conviction rise up in his heart:

Worth it.

Only a vision like this one, of Jesus standing by the throne to receive you home, can give you the power to go the distance.

Sometimes in church we talk about Jesus as the missing piece in our lives, our guide, our help in time of trouble. And he is all those things. But the only thing that will compel the kind of obedience we see in Stephen is a vision of Jesus standing alone at the end, victorious over it all.

You have to decide if knowing him, and being received by him, is by itself worth it.

You see, if you're really serious about following Jesus, at some point obedience to him is going to take you 180 degrees opposite the direction that you think you want to go. In that moment you have to decide if obedience to him is worth it.

Who is going to be waiting around the throne to receive you home?

Our families are precious. Our friends are a blessing. Our dreams are important. But none of those things will be waiting for us around the throne, and, thus, none are worthy of the offering of our lives.

Only Jesus is.

Clara

Clara was a young woman who moved to a remote part of Central Asia to work alongside one of our mission teams there. For five years she served the poorest of the poor.

Late one night in January of 2008, Clara was kidnapped by Muslim extremists. They perceived her presence there as a threat.

She brought education to women, whom they believed should not learn skills outside the home. And, she was a Christian.

Clara had left a very comfortable life in the American Southeast to live in a place where dust storms were a daily occurrence; where windows require blast film because of the constant risk of bomb explosions; where sometimes there is no electricity to run even a fan in the midst of 100-degree heat; where she had only sporadic internet access to get news from home; and where an armed Islamic group that is hostile to the gospel operates with impunity. Clara did all of this because she understood that Christ had come to earth to face even greater dangers for her. She did it joyfully.

Our team leader negotiated with the hostage-takers for six months. They kept moving her from location to location. United States Special Forces tried several rescue attempts, and twice they got very close. On one occasion, she was rushed into a neighboring house just before the troops arrived. On another, she was hidden in the floorboards of a house that the troops were searching. I can only imagine what Clara must have felt to hear her rescuers just a few feet away, unable to get their attention.

When news of her kidnapping was heard in the streets, women from the southern stronghold of these Islamic extremists were outraged. Something unheard of happened: three hundred women marched to the governor's mansion to demand that he do something to free her. These women had benefited from Clara's projects. They didn't fully understand the gospel yet, but they had seen Christ in Clara.

I wish I could say there was a happy ending to this story, but we don't ultimately know what happened to Clara. She kept being moved from village to village, handed off from one group of rogue Islamists to another. The last we heard, she had been taken by a nomadic group of arms smugglers across a Central Asian desert.

And then the trail went cold. We don't know for sure if she was killed. The kidnappers said they were going to kill her because she was a Christian, and at this point, we have to conclude they carried through with their threat. Still, we have no proof and no body.

I asked our team leader, who led in the negotiations, if Clara was an extraordinary hero of faith. He replied,

> Well, in a sense, now we see that she was. But when I think about her, I remember a regular girl from the American South, a smiling friend, a person who struggled like the rest of us when it was hot; a girl who loved to go on vacation; a regular American girl who decided to step out in faith and obey a calling from Jesus to go to a place that she wasn't sure she could handle.
>
> I saw God's grace and strength enable Clara to set up an amazing project here in Central Asia. It's a grace that got the attention of the community, and I am sure that same grace and strength were with her when she was taken by the Muslim extremists.

He then paused, thought for a moment, and said:

> Faith is demonstrated in times of adversity,
> but its reality is manifested long before that.
> Sometimes faith is quiet, working humbly in
> love, but that is the same faith that makes a
> regular girl like Clara stand up to one of his-
> tory's most vicious regimes and say, "No. Christ
> is better. You can take my life, but you can't
> take him. His mission will outlive all of us."

Worth it.

A Wasted Life or a Worthy One?

If you live a life of radical obedience, not everyone is going to praise you. Many whom you love and trust will question your motives. And because you threaten the status quo, you should be prepared to deal with opposition from places you never expected it. From friends. For some, from your parents. Religious leaders. Some will act like in obeying him you are betraying *them*.

That's why you have to keep your eyes fixed firmly on the One beside the throne, the One standing ready to receive you home.

Because his standing ovation outweighs their scorn. He's worth it.

In 1904, William Borden graduated from high school. He was the heir to the Borden family fortune. At the time, the Borden Milk Company was one of the most profitable businesses in the United States, which would have made young William one of the richest men in the country. Upon graduation, his parents gave him a luxurious graduation gift—a trip across the globe.

Something happened on that trip, however, that his parents were not anticipating. Borden became overwhelmed by the world's lostness. He couldn't get over the masses of people with no chance of hearing the gospel. Borden was a new believer, and he wanted to do something about it.

William told his father that he didn't want to take on the family business. He wanted to be a missionary. His parents were furious, but William told them that he would divert any inheritance he received into the mission. Some of William's Christian friends even told him, "You're throwing everything away. You're wasting your life!"

But Borden wouldn't be dissuaded. After graduating from the University of Yale and then Princeton Seminary, he climbed aboard a boat headed for China.

Because Borden intended to work with Muslims in China, he stopped in Egypt to spend time learning Arabic. One month after arriving, however, he contracted spinal meningitis and died. He was twenty-five years old.

Back in the United States headlines proclaimed the tragic news. The stories echoed the advice Borden's friends and family had given him: *What a waste of a life!*

But Borden didn't think so. As the story goes, while on his deathbed, someone asked if he had any final words. He pulled out his Bible, turned to a blank page at the back, and wrote, "No regrets."

From the perspective of the world, Borden's life was wasted. From the perspective of eternity, it wasn't. His was not a wasted life, but a worthy one.

William Borden is buried in a small cemetery in Cairo. The cemetery is so out of the way that if you don't know what you are looking for, you'll never find it. His tombstone is bunched up among many others, and the writing on it is so faint you can barely read it. But if you get down real close you can make out a single sentence: *"Apart from faith in Christ, there is no explanation for such a life."*

Apart from faith in Christ, there is no explanation for such a life.

Will that be true of *your* life?

What are you going to do with your life? Are you going to use it in a way that only makes sense if eternity is real and the gospel is true?

We have to make up our minds: If Christ is risen, then nothing invested into his kingdom is ever wasted. If he's risen, everything we invest anywhere else is.

Only one life to live, 'twill soon be past. Only what's done for Christ will last.

Do you believe this?

Will you adopt it as your personal credo?

If you do, then live in such a way that it will one day be said of you: *Apart from faith in Christ, there is no explanation of such a life.*

Because only by a life lived like that will you be able to say in the end:

Worth it.

Put Your "Yes" on the Table

Imagine receiving a letter like this from someone wanting to marry your daughter:

> *I have now to ask, whether you can consent to part with your daughter early next spring, to see her no more in this world, whether you can consent to her departure to a heathen land, and her subjection to the hardships and sufferings of a missionary life? Whether you can consent to her exposure to the dangers of the ocean; to the fatal influence of the southern climate of India; to every kind of want and distress; to degradation, insult, persecution, and perhaps a violent death?*
>
> *Can you consent to all this, for the sake of him who left his heavenly home and died for her and for you; for the sake of perishing, immortal souls;*

for the sake of Zion and the glory of God? Can
you consent to all this, in hope of soon meeting
your daughter in the world of glory, with a crown
of righteousness brightened by the acclamations
of praise which shall resound to her Saviour from
the lost who were saved, through her means, from
eternal woe and despair?

This was the letter that Adoniram Judson, one of America's first foreign missionaries, sent to his prospective father-in-law, John Hasseltine, asking for his daughter Ann's hand in marriage. Amazingly, John gave his consent.

Adoniram Judson's biography was the first book I read after becoming a Christian at age sixteen. His testimony of complete abandon for the gospel stirred me deeply.

It was later that same year that I sat in an audience of several hundred high school students at the Word of Life Island in Schroon Lake, New York, where Paul Bubar challenged us to come forward, grab a stick that symbolically represented our lives, and throw it into the fire. As our stick disintegrated into wisps of smoke, we were to reflect on whether we were willing for God to do that with our lives.

I sat there in the audience, heart beating wildly. I knew I wanted my life to count. I knew I didn't want to waste it. I wanted to live without regrets.

I stepped out, timidly at first, but gaining confidence with every step. I grabbed a stick and threw it in.

I stood by the fire a few moments to watch it burn, then I turned around and went back to my seat. I have never looked back, and never once regretted it.

> *Only one life to live, 'twill soon be past. Only*
> *what's done for Christ will last.*

Adoniram Judson and Ann Hassletine were married on February 5, 1812, and left for India (and ultimately Burma) that same year. Ann never returned, passing into eternity in 1826, a victim of the long, dreadful months of disease, death, stress, and loneliness that had been her station for twenty-one months. Adoniram and Ann's third child died six months after Ann. In other words, most of the things Adoniram warned his prospective father-in-law about came true.

A wasted life?

When Adoniram Judson arrived in Burma in 1813, there were no Christians. Today, Burma (Myanmar) has more than 2 million Baptists (not even counting other Christians), the third most of any country in the world.[1]

> "Truly I tell you, unless a grain of wheat falls to
> the ground and dies, it remains by itself. But if
> it dies, it produces much fruit." (John 12:24)

I have a feeling that somewhere from eternity he and Ann are looking down and saying, "Worth it."

I, for one, hope to join them.

I hope you will, too.

It starts by putting your "yes" on the table, and letting God put it on the map.

Are you ready to do that?

Where Do I Go from Here?

The Go2 Challenge

Where do you go from here? What do you do if you've read this book and you want to make your life worth it, but you don't know where to start?

I'll ask you the same question I ask every college graduate at The Summit Church.

You've got to get a job somewhere. Why not get a job in a place where God is doing something strategic?

We challenge our college graduates to let the mission of God be the most significant factor in determining where and how they pursue their careers. We challenge them to dedicate the first two years after they graduate to join a church planting team working somewhere in North America or around the globe. We call it the "Go2 Challenge."

Give us two years and we'll change the world. We sometimes refer to this, tongue-in-cheek, as "the Mormonization strategy."

Just kidding. But seriously, if Mormons can do this for a works-based gospel, can't we do it for the real one?

If you are reading this book wondering about a next step, let me challenge you to consider this one: take the Go2 Challenge.

Whether you are in college considering what God has for you next, at a transitional point in your career, or nearing retirement, why not consider investing two years directly into the mission of God?

Give two years! It will change the world.

Here's a few concerns and questions you might have:

"But I'm Not a College Student."

While I often lead out in this challenge talking to college students, this isn't just a challenge for them. The second most "sendable" group of people in our church are retirees. *Forbes* magazine notes that most Americans' retirement will last twenty years, with the possibility of it lasting up to thirty. What might it look like for the demographic with the most life experience and spiritual maturity to invest that wisdom into young men and women on church planting teams?

So if you're retiring, I'll issue the same challenge: give at least the first two years of retirement to living on mission for God.

Give two years! It will change the world.

"Won't Going for Two Years Mess Up My Career?"

College students sometimes ask me, "If I pause my career for two years, won't I be behind?"

Well, first, who says you have to *pause* it? The idea is that perhaps you can *pursue* your career in a location where you can be a part of a church plant.

But even if you do pause it, like I did, it likely won't set you back. If anything, it likely will help it.

Look through the biographies of CEOs of Fortune 500 companies, and you'll find that many of them had a post-college stint in the military or the Peace Corps. Living intentionally on mission, particularly in a challenging context, builds character in ways that no internship or apprenticeship can. These settings yield lifelong benefits. A friend of mine, who oversees one of the largest college scholarship and young leadership development programs in America, recently told me, "There's a reason Mormons are so disproportionately represented in the upper echelons of business leadership. A lot of it goes back to the character development that takes place in their two-year mission."

After being on a team like this for a couple of years, God may lead you to plant your life there permanently. That's what happens to many of those we send from our church. Others return knowing they gave the first and best of their careers to God, something God surely will bless. Jesus said, after all, "Seek first the kingdom of God and his righteousness, and all these things will be provided for you" (Matt. 6:33). That verse applies to your career, too.

In fact, you might think of this two-year challenge like "tithing" your career—giving to God its firstfruits. And, as with every other area in which you give God your first and best, watch how God uses that commitment of faith to bless you.

If you are a college student, this time in life affords you some unique opportunities. You are less encumbered now than you will ever be again in your life. Don't live your life wondering what *might have* happened had you put the Great Commission first in your career choice! If after two years God sends you back to your hometown, at least you'll know that you are sent there, and your understanding of what God is doing around the world will be permanently transformed.

"Do I Need to Leave Behind My Job?"

Maybe. For many, you will be able to find a job in your career field in one of these places. If so, you'll be able to go without having to raise money. Financially, you'll be a net-positive for the mission!

But, as we discussed in chapter 3, God may lead you to leave behind your work and devote yourself entirely to the work of the ministry.

God calls some to *leverage* their careers and for others to *leave* them. At our church, we call this the "leverage or leave?" question: Is God calling you to leverage your career for the Great Commission, like the Moravians, or to leave it behind, like

William Carey, Adoniram Judson, and Lottie Moon? He leads his followers both directions.

"How Can I Find Out about Opportunities?"

Great question. In the denomination our church participates in (the Southern Baptist Convention), the North American Mission Board has established fifty "Send Cities" that are under-churched and in which they can help partner you with a new church plant.

Additionally, our International Mission Board has a number of two-year programs that can place you on a team serving somewhere overseas in the least reached places on earth.

Your denomination or local church probably has its own connections. Groups like Cru, Frontiers, Campus Outreach, and Radical have cross-denominational opportunities you can access as well.

If all that sounds too tough, just move to Raleigh and join The Summit Church. We'll send you out from here! Kidding. Sort of. I mean, we won't turn you away. Just come on over and we'll figure it out.

You can find out more about these (and other) options at go2years.net.

"But I Feel Called to Be a Pastor/Work in a Church in America."

Okay, well why not consider *leading* an English-speaking church overseas? One of the most underdeveloped and under-served outlets of ministry are international churches in big cities around the world. Christian businessmen and women moving to cities like Berlin, Moscow, Dubai, Cairo, Kuala Lumpur, Singapore, and London need gospel-centered, mission-focused churches to plug into, churches that can help train and support them in local mission.

Often in those churches you find not only expatriates from the United States and other Western countries but also motivated and highly successful English-speaking nationals. Because these nationals can relate to both Western culture and their indigenous ones, they can be key in reaching the rest of the country. You can help reach the ones who will reach the rest of the country.

So, if God has called you to lead a church, why not consider serving a church in a much-less-reached country?

Give two years! It'll change the world.

I hope you'll get the conversation started at go2years.net.

Notes

Chapter 1: Don't Waste Your Life

1. John Piper, "Boasting Only in the Cross," sermon delivered May 20, 2000, Memphis, Tennessee, Passion's OneDay 2000, https://www.desiringgod.org/messages/boasting-only-in-the-cross.

2. Matt Carter, August 23, 2016, https://twitter.com/_Matt_Carter/status/768290293724491776.

3. Trevin Wax, "John Piper Is Not Anti-Seashell," May 20, 2013, https://www.thegospelcoalition.org/blogs/trevin-wax/john-piper-is-not-anti-seashell/.

4. Sarah Eekhoff Zylstra, "How John Piper's Seashells Swept Over a Generation," https://www.thegospelcoalition.org/article/how-john-pipers-seashells-swept-over-a-generation/.

5. Ibid.

6. "Transcript: Tom Brady, Part 3," *60 Minutes*, https://www.cbsnews.com/news/transcript-tom-brady-part-3/; "Tom Brady on Winning: There's Got to Be More Than This," https://www.youtube.com/watch?v=-TA4_fVkv3c.

7. "Full Speech Jim Carrey's Commencement Address at the 2014 MUM Graduation (EN, FR, ES, RU, GR, . . .)," speech delivered May 28, 2014; Fairfield, Iowa, Maharishi University of Management Graduation, https://www.youtube.com/watch?v=V80-gPkpH6M.

8. "Millennials: Big Career Goals, Limited Job Prospects," Barna Group, June 10, 2014, https://www.barna.com/research/millennials-big-career-goals-limited-job-prospects/.

9. Trevin Wax, "Piper: Care About Suffering Now, Especially Eternal Suffering Later," February 3, 2011, https://www.thegospel coalition.org/blogs/trevin-wax/piper-care-about-all-suffering-now-especially-eternal-suffering-later/.

10. "Ego pro te haec passus sum. Tu vero quid fecisti pro me?"

11. William Danker writes, ". . . [T]hese business enterprises [of the Moravians] were the rockets that hoisted pioneer Moravian satellites into the missionary heavens in an age when other Protestants were doing next to nothing." *Profit for the Lord: Economic Activities in Moravian Missions and the Basel Mission Trading Company* (Eugene, OR: Wipf and Stock, 1971), 72–73.

12. "Report of the First International Convention of the Student Volunteer Movement for Foreign Missions" (Boston, MA: T.O. Metcalf, 1891), 12.

13. Norman Grubb, *C. T. Studd, Athlete and Pioneer* (Grand Rapids, MI: Zondervan, 1946), 129.

14. Piper, "Boasting Only in the Cross," https://www.desiringgod.org/messages/boasting-only-in-the-cross.

15. Norman Grubb, *C. T. Studd, Athlete and Pioneer.*

16. Justin Taylor, "He Was No Fool," January 19, 2020, https://www.thegospelcoalition.org/blogs/justin-taylor/he-ws-no-fool/.

17. C. T. Studd, "Only One Life to Live," (n.d.).

Chapter 2: Kick Your Bucket List

1. N. T. Wright, *Simply Christian: Why Christianity Makes Sense* (New York, NY: HarperOne, 2010), 186.

2. C. S. Lewis, *The Last Battle,* Chronicles of Narnia (1956; repr., New York, NY: HarperCollins, 2005), 208, 213, 230.

3. Ibid.

4. Said in the live conference performance of "Asleep in the Light," as recorded on his *Keith Green's Greatest Hits.*

5. Referenced in James Limburg, *Psalms,* Westminster Bible Companion (Louisville, KY: Westminster John Knox, 2000), 310.

6. Trevor Haynes, "Dopamine, Smartphones and You: A Battle for Your Time," May 1, 2018, http://sitn.hms.harvard.edu/flash/2018/dopamine-smartphones-battle-time/.

7. "How Many People Die Every Single Minute," January 31, 2018, http://www.quora.com/How-many-people-die-every-single-minute.

8. Elisabeth Elliot, *Shadow of the Almighty: The Life and Testament of Jim Elliot* (Peabody, MA: Hendrickson, 1958), 182–83.

Chapter 3: The Myth of Calling

1. Genesis 19:26

2. Irenaeus, *Against Heresies*, 3:12:8 (AD 180).

3. Stephen Neill, *History of Christian Missions* (1964, repr., New York, NY: Penguin Books, 1990), 22.

4. Mike Barnett, *Discovering the Mission of God Supplement* (Downers Grove, IL: InterVarsity Press, 2012).

5. Rodney Stark, *The Rise of Christianity* (Princeton, NJ: Princeton University Press, 1996), 161.

6. Origen, *Against Celsus,* 3.10.

7. Stark, *The Rise of Christianity,* 5–8.

8. Francis Chan, *Letters to the Church* (Colorado Springs, CO: David C Cook, 2018), 120.

Chapter 4: Greater Than John

1. Though the ministry of John the Baptist is recorded in the New Testament, his preaching was done under the auspices of the old covenant. Like all Old Testament prophets, his preaching pointed toward the coming salvation of Jesus.

2. Furthermore, our "works" would be greater in that they would facilitate a miracle greater than the effect of any of Jesus' healing miracles. Whereas making the lame walk and even raising the dead were only temporary solutions to human brokenness, the salvation they pointed to is eternal. Thus, introducing someone to the salvation that Jesus' miracles only signified is a "greater" and more long-lasting work than even Jesus' healings were.

For more on this, see my book *Jesus, Continued . . . : Why the Spirit Inside You Is Better Than Jesus Beside You* (Grand Rapids, MI: Zondervan, 2014).

3. The question of how we should hear the voice of the Holy Spirit and follow him is more important—and complex—than I can deal with here. I wrote a previous book, *Jesus, Continued . . .* that dives into that question. I would also recommend Kevin DeYoung's *Just Do Something* and Henry Blackaby's *Experiencing God*. For a more robust treatment of the topic, I recommend Wayne Grudem's chapter on the guidance of the Holy Spirit in his *Systematic Theology* and Malcolm Yarnell's chapter in the volume edited by Danny Akin, *Theology for the Church*.

4. John Newton, "Letter IV: Communion with God," in *The Letters of John Newton* (Edinburgh: Banner of Truth Trust, 1960), 29.

5. Gary Tyra, *The Holy Spirit in Mission: Prophetic Speech and Action in Christian Witness* (Downers Grove, IL: IVP Academic, 2011).

Chapter 5: The Law of the Harvest

1. I originally shared this story in *Gaining by Losing* (Grand Rapids, MI: Zondervan, 2015).

2. Ishmael, of course, is also a son, but not regarded as a son of promise (Heb. 11:17).

3. Keith Green, "Last Days Ministries: Keith Green," n.d., https://www.lastdaysministries.org/Groups/1000008644/Last_Days_Ministries/Keith_Green/Keith_Green.aspx.

4. Matthew 25:15 ESV

Chapter 6: One Thing You Lack

1. C. S. Lewis, *Mere Christianity* (1952; repr., San Francisco, CA: HarperSanFrancisco, 2001), 56.

2. Flannery O'Connor, *Wise Blood* (New York, NY: Farrar, Straus and Giroux, 1962), 16.

3. John Piper, *What Jesus Demands from the World* (Wheaton, IL: Crossway, 2006), 154.

Chapter 7: Audience of One

1. John Piper, *What Jesus Demands from the World* (Wheaton, IL: Crossway, 2006), 287.

2. *The Collected Letters of C. S. Lewis,* vol, 3, Narnia, Cambridge, and Joy, 1950–1963, ed. Walter Hooper (San Francisco, CA: HarperSanFrancisco, 2007), 111.

3. Corrie Ten Boom, *The Hiding Place* (1971; repr., Peabody, MA: Hendrickson Publishers, 2009), x.

4. C. S. Lewis, *The Weight of Glory* (1949; repr., New York, NY: HarperOne, 2001), 30–31.

5. The more literal translation of Polycarp's words: "You threaten me with fire which burns for an hour, and after a little is extinguished, but are ignorant of the fire of the coming judgment and of eternal punishment, reserved for the ungodly. But why do you tarry? Bring forth what you will." "The Martyrdom of Polycarp," in *Ante-Nicene Fathers*, eds. A. Cleveland Coxe, James Donaldson, and Alexander Roberts (Buffalo, NY: Christian Literature, 1885), accessed via http://www.newadvent.org/fathers/0102.htm.

Chapter 8: Do People Really Need to Hear about Jesus to Get to Heaven?

1. I am indebted to David Platt for much of the framework of this chapter. While I am following Paul's argument in Romans rather closely, the specific framing of these premises was inspired by Platt in *Radical: Taking Back Your Faith from the American Dream* (Colorado Springs, CO: Multnomah Books, 2010), 145–64. Platt says he is following R. C. Sproul, who apparently took it right from Paul.

2. Mary Lowe Dickinson and Myrta Lockett Avary, *Heaven, Home and Happiness* (New York, NY: The Christian Herald, 1901), 216.

3. Tim Keller, "The Disobedience of Saul," sermon preached at Redeemer Presbyterian Church on January 4, 2004, http://www.gospelin-life.com/downloads/the-disobedience-of-saul/.

4. Quoted by Danny Akin and Walter Strickland in *The SBC and the 21st Century: Reflection, Renewal & Recommitment,* ed. Jason K. Allen (Nashville, TN: B&H Academic, 2019), 203.

5. Some theologians even have a name for this: the "anonymous Christian." See eds. Karl Rahner, Paul Imhof, and Hubert Biallowons, trans. Harvey D. Egan, *Karl Rahner in Dialogue: Conversations and Interviews, 1965–1982* (New York, NY: Crossroad, 1986), 207.

6. A term coined by Karl Rahner, the Jesuit theologian who popularized the idea at the Second Vatican Council that many people who have never heard about Jesus can still be saved through an "implicit faith" they gain from creation.

7. Todd Ahrend, *In This Generation: Looking to the Past to Reach the Present* (Portland, OR: Dawson Media, 2010), 125.

Epilogue: Put Your "Yes" on the Table

1. Tobin Perry, "Adoniram Judson's Spiritual Descendants in Massachusetts, December 9, 2019, http://www.bpnews.net/54026/adoniram-judsons-spiritual-descendants-in-massachusetts.

also available
from **J. D. GREEAR**

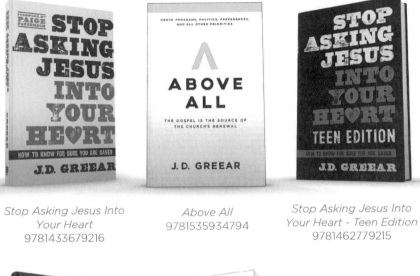

Stop Asking Jesus Into Your Heart
9781433679216

Above All
9781535934794

Stop Asking Jesus Into Your Heart - Teen Edition
9781462779215

Gospel Journal
9781535934817

Gospel
9781433673122

Gospel Devotional
9781535934657

Available where books are sold.